IMITATIONS

D1040476

Books by Robert Lowell

COLLECTED PROSE (1987)
THE ORESTEIA OF AESCHYLUS (1978)
DAY BY DAY (1977)
SELECTED POEMS (1976)
THE DOLPHIN (1973)
HISTORY (1973)
FOR LIZZIE AND HARRIET (1973)
NOTEBOOK (1969)
(REVISED AND EXPANDED EDITION, 1970)
PROMETHEUS BOUND (1969)
THE VOYAGE & OTHER VERSIONS
OF POEMS BY BAUDELAIRE (1969)
NEAR THE OCEAN (1967)
THE OLD GLORY (1965)
FOR THE UNION DEAD (1964)
IMITATIONS (1961)
PHAEDRA (TRANSLATION) (1961)
LIFE STUDIES (1959)
THE MILLS OF THE KAVANAUGHS (1951)
LORD WEARY'S CASTLE (1946)
LAND OF UNLIKENESS (1944)

Robert Lowell

IMITATIONS

THE NOONDAY PRESS
Farrar, Straus and Giroux
New York

Copyright © 1958, 1959, 1960, 1961 by
Robert Lowell © renewed 1986, 1987, 1989 by
Caroline Lowell, Harriet Lowell, and Sheridan Lowell
First published in 1961 by Farrar, Straus and Giroux
This edition first published in 1990 by
The Noonday Press
Published in Canada by HarperCollins*CanadaLtd*
Printed in the United States of America
Library of Congress catalog card number: 61–13679
Drawing on title-page
by Frank Parker

Contents

ix

Introduction

This book is partly self-sufficient and separate from its sources, and should be first read as a sequence, one voice running through many personalities, contrasts and repetitions. I have hoped somehow for a whole, to make a single volume, a small anthology of European poetry. The dark and against the grain stand out, but there are other modifying strands. I have tried to keep something equivalent to the fire and finish of my originals. This has forced me to do considerable re-writing.

Boris Pasternak has said that the usual reliable translator gets the literal meaning but misses the tone, and that in poetry tone is of course everything. I have been reckless with literal meaning, and labored hard to get the tone. Most often this has been *a* tone, for *the* tone is something that will always more or less escape transference to another language and cultural moment. I have tried to write alive English and to do what my authors might have done if they were writing their poems now and in America.

Most poetic translations come to grief and are less enjoyable than modest photographic prose translations, such as George Kay has offered in his *Penguin Book of Italian Verse*. Strict metrical translators still exist. They seem to live in a pure world untouched by contemporary poetry. Their difficulties are bold and honest, but they are taxidermists, not poets, and their poems are likely to be stuffed birds. A better strategy would seem to be the now fashionable translations into free or irregular verse. Yet this method commonly turns out a sprawl of language, neither faithful nor distinguished, now on stilts, now low, as

Dryden would say. It seems self-evident that no professor or amateur poet, or even good poet writing hastily, can by miracle transform himself into a fine metricist. I believe that poetic translation—I would call it an imitation—must be expert and inspired, and needs at least as much technique, luck and rightness of hand as an original poem.

My licenses have been many. My first two Sappho poems are really new poems based on hers. Villon has been somewhat stripped; Hebel is taken out of dialect; Hugo's "Gautier" is cut in half. Mallarmé has been unclotted, not because I disapprove of his dense medium but because I saw no way of giving it much power in English. The same has been done with Ungaretti and some of the more obscure Rimbaud. About a third of "The Drunken Boat" has been left out. Two stanzas have been added to Rilke's "Roman Sarcophagus," and one to his "Pigeons." "Pigeons" and Valéry's "Helen" are more idiomatic and informal in my English. Some lines from Villon's "Little Testament" have been shifted to introduce his "Great Testament." And so forth! I have dropped lines, moved lines, moved stanzas, changed images and altered meter and intent.

Pasternak has given me special problems. From reading his prose and many translations of his poetry, I have come to feel that he is a very great poet. But I know no Russian. I have rashly tried to improve on other translations, and have been helped by exact prose versions given me by Russian readers. This is an old practice; Pasternak himself, I think, worked this way with his Georgian poets. I hope I caught something worthy of his all-important tone.

This book was written from time to time when I was unable to do anything of my own. It began some ten years ago when I read a parallel French translation of Rilke's "Orpheus," and felt that a much better job might be done in English. I had long been amazed by Montale, but had no idea how he might be worked until I saw that unlike most good poets—Horace and Petrarch are extremes—he was strong in simple prose and could be made still stronger in free verse.

My Baudelaires were begun as exercises in couplets and quatrains and to get away from the longer, less concentrated problems of translating Racine's *Phèdre*.

All my originals are important poems. Nothing like them exists in English, for the excellence of a poet depends on the unique opportunities of his native language. I have been almost as free as the authors themselves in finding ways to make them ring right for me.

—ROBERT LOWELL

Acknowledgements

I have been so free with my texts that it is perhaps an impertinence for me to thank those people, more expert in languages than I, for their scattered help. Corrections in my Italian were made by Alfredo Rizzardi and Renato Poggioli; in my French by Jackson Mathews, T. S. Eliot and Elizabeth Bishop; in my German by Hannah Arendt. Russian trots were given me by Mrs. Roman Jakobson, Mrs. Olga Carlisle and Nicolas Nabokov. Swarms of published translations were useful and irritating to me. General stylistic suggestions were made by my wife, Stanley Kunitz, Mary McCarthy, William Alfred, I. A. Richards, Adrienne Rich and William Meredith.

Acknowledgements are also due the editors of the following publications in which some of the poems first appeared: *Art News, The Atlantic, Catholic Worker, Encounter, Harper's, Harper's Bazaar, Harvard Advocate, Hudson Review, Kenyon Review, The Nation, The Observer, Paris Review, Poetry,* and *Quarterly Review of Literature;* and to Edizione della Lanterna, Bologna, who first published my Montales.

R. L.

FOR ELIZABETH BISHOP

IMITATIONS

The Killing of Lykaon

Sing for me, Muse, the mania of Achilles
that cast a thousand sorrows on the Greeks
and threw so many huge souls into hell,
heroes who spilled their lives as food for dogs
and darting birds. God's will was working out,
from that time when first fell apart fighting
Atrides, king of men, and that god, Achilles . . .

*　　*　　*

"Coward, do not speak to me of ransom!
Before the day of terror overtook Patroklos,
sparing Trojans was my heart's choice and rest—
thousands I seized alive and sold like sheep!
Now there's not one who'll run out with his life,
should the god throw him to me before Troy,
but none are more accursed than Priam's sons . . .
You too must die, my dear. Why do you care?
Patroklos, a much better man, has died.
Or look at me —how large and fine I am—
a goddess bore me, and my father reigned,
yet I too have my destiny and death:
either at sunrise, night, or at high noon,
some warrior will spear me down in the lines,
or stick me with an arrow through the heel."

He spoke so, and Lykaon lost his heart,
his spear dropped, and he fluttered his two hands
begging Achilles to hold back his sword.
The sword bit through his neck and collarbone,
and flashed blue sky. His face fell in the dust,
the black blood spouted out, and soaked the earth.

Achilles hurled Lykaon by his heel
in the Skamander, and spoke these wingéd words:
"Lie with the fish, they'll dress your wounds, and lick
away your blood, and have no care for you,
nor will your mother groan beside your pyre
by the Skamander, nor will women wail
as you swirl down the rapids to the sea,
but the dark shadows of the fish will shiver,
lunging to snap Lykaon's silver fat.
Die, Trojans—you must die till I reach Troy—
you'll run in front, I'll scythe you down behind,
nor will the azure Skamander save your lives,
whirling and silver, though you kill your bulls
and sheep, and throw a thousand one-hoofed horse,
still living, in the ripples. You must die,
and die and die and die, until the blood
of Hellas and Patroklos is avenged,
killed by the running ships when I was gone."

Homer: *Iliad,* from Bks. I and **XXI.**

Three Letters to Anaktoria

[*The man or hero loves Anaktoria, later Sappho;
in the end, he withdraws or dies.*]

I

I set that man above the gods and heroes—
all day, he sits before you face to face,
like a cardplayer. Your elbow brushes his elbow—
if you should speak, he hears.

The touched heart madly stirs,
your laughter is water hurrying over pebbles—
every gesture is a proclamation,
every sound is speech . . .

Refining fire purifies my flesh!
I hear you: a hollowness in my ears
thunders and stuns me. I cannot speak.
I cannot see.

I shiver. A dead whiteness spreads over
my body, trickling pinpricks of sweat.
I am greener than the greenest green grass—
I die!

For some the fairest thing on the dark earth is Thermopylae
and the Spartan phalanx lowering lances to die—
Salamis and the half-moon of Athenian triremes
sprinting to pin down the Persian fleet;
nothing is as fair as my beloved.

I can easily make you understand this:
dwell on the gentleness of his footstep,
the shimmer of his shining face fairer than ten thousand
barbarous scythe-wheeled Persian chariots,
or the myriad hanging gardens in Persepolis.

Helen forgot her husband and dear children
to cherish Paris,
the loveliest of mortals,
the murderer of Troy—
she bestowed her heart far off.

How easily a woman is led astray!
She remembers nothing of what is nearest at hand:
her loom, her household, her helots . . .
Anaktoria, did you cherish my love,
when the Bridegroom was with you?

A woman seldom finds what is best—
no, never in this world,
Anaktoria! Pray
for his magnificence I once pined to share . . .
to have lived is better than to live!

III

The moon slides west,
it is midnight,
the time is gone—
I lie alone!

Sappho.

Children

Years back here we were children
and at the stage of running
in gangs about the meadows—
here to this one, there to that one.
Where we picked up violets
on lucky days,
you can now see cattle gadding about.

I still remember hunching
ankle deep in violets,
squabbling over which bunches were fairest.
Our childishness was obvious—
we ran dancing rounds,
we wore new green wreaths.
So time passes.

Here we ran swilling strawberries
from oak to pine,
through hedges, through turnstiles—
as long as day was burning down.
Once a gardener
rushed from an arbor:
"O. K. now, children, run home."

We came out in spots
those yesterdays, when we stuffed on strawberries;
it was just a childish game to us.
Often we heard
the herdsman
hooing and warning us:
"Children, the woods are alive with snakes."

And one of the children breaking
through the sharp grass, grew white
and shouted, "Children, a snake
ran in there. He got our pony.
She'll never get well.
I wish that snake
would go to hell!"

"Well then, get out of the woods!
If you don't hurry away quickly,
I'll tell you what will happen—
if you don't leave the forest
behind you by daylight,
you'll lose yourselves;
your pleasure will end in bawling."

Do you know how five virgins
dawdled in the meadow,
till the king slammed his dining-room door?
Their shouting and shame were outrageous:
their jailer tore everything off them,
down to their skins
they stood like milk cows without any clothes.

Der Wilde Alexander: *Hie vor dô wir kinder wâren.*

The Great Testament

(*For William Carlos Williams*)

I am thirty this year,
near Christmas, the dead season,
when wolves live off the wind,
and the poor peasants fear
the icy firmament.
Sound in body and mind,
I write my Testament,
but the ink has frozen.

Where are those gallant men
I ran with in my youth?
They sang and spoke so well!
Ah nothing can survive
after the last amen;
some are perhaps in hell.
May they sleep in God's truth;
God save those still alive!

Some have risen—are grave
merchants, lords, divines;
some only see bread, when
it's out of reach in windows;
others have taken vows:
Carthusians, Celestines,
wear boots like oyster men—
what different lives men have!

These mighty men—God grant
they do good works, increase,
and live in charity—
who will correct the great?
But the poor are like me,
they've nothing. They can wait—
the gods take what they want,
and eat their bread and cheese.

I have loved—all I could!—
when I try love again,
diseases ring like bells
through my liver and blood,
and warn me off this road.
Sell love to someone else,
who puts away more food—
dancing's for fatter men!

If I had studied, God,
in my youth's day of joy,
and lived by book and rule,
I would have slept in down;
but I ran off from school,
like a delinquent boy—
my heart swims in its blood,
when I must write this down!

I took the preacher's text
too much for Gospel truth:
"In the light of your eyes,
rejoice and have your wish!"
In the verse coming next,
he serves another dish:
"What are childhood and youth,
but vanity and vice?"

How quickly my youth went,
like ravellings of cloth
the weaver holds to cut
with wisps of burning straws!
Kinsmen, kinswomen, both—
I tell the truth—now cut
me when I pass, because
I have no goods or rent.

I think now of those skulls
piling up in the morgue—
all masters of the rolls,
or the king's treasurers,
or water-carriers,
or blacksmiths at the forge.
Who'll tell me which is which,
which poor, and which were rich?

And there are women here,
who used to bow and scrape,
and struggle for earth's joys;
some of them gave commands,
and others served in fear.
I see that none escape:
bishops, laymen, or boys!
They rot with folded hands.

They're dead, God rest their souls!
These poor corpses were once
kings, princes of the blood,
living on tender food,
puddings and creams and rice—
no one laughs out or cries;
the dust eats up their bones.
Jesus, absolve their souls! . . .

Ah God, the days I lost!
Youth and what I loved most
went when my back was turned!
Old age came limping on—
I was less ripe than black!
nothing left on horseback
or foot, alas! What then?
My life suddenly burned.

I descend from no name—
poor from my mother's womb,
poverty claws me down.
My father was poor; Horace,
his father, was the same—
on my ancestors' tomb,
God rest their souls! there is
neither scepter nor crown.

When I curse poverty,
often my heart tells me,
Villon, why do you give
poverty so much room?
Though you've less than Jacques Coeur,
men in cheap cloth still live—
why play the grand seigneur
to rot in a rich tomb?

Poor has-been lords, you die,
you are lords no more. Look,
King David's Psalter says,
"their place forgets their name."
I'll let the rest go by,
it's not my business—
teaching preachers the book
is not my trade and game.

What more have I to tell?
I'm no arch-angel's heir,
crowned with the stars and moon.
My father (God have mercy!)
is in the ground, and soon
my mother also must die—
poor soul, she knows it well,
her son must follow her.

I know that rich and base,
priests, laymen, clerks and sots,
lords, bishops, serfs and thieves,
beautiful, squat or tall,
ladies with ermined sleeves,
and men of every class,
in cone or horse-hair hats . . .
Who else? Death takes them all.

Helen has paid this debt—
no one who dies dies well:
breath goes, and your eyes too,
your spleen bursts through your life,
then sweat . . . God knows . . . you sweat!
No mother, child or wife
wishes to die for you,
and suffer your last hell.

Who cares then to die shriven?
Feet cramp, the nostrils curve,
eyes stare, the stretched veins hiss
and ache through joint and nerve—
Oh woman's body, poor,
supple, tender—is this
what you were waiting for?
Yes, or ascend to heaven.

Villon: *Le grand testament*

Ballad for the Dead Ladies

Say in what land, or where
is Flora, the lovely Roman,
Andromeda, or Helen,
far lovelier,
or Echo, who would answer
across the brook or river—
her beauty was more than human!
Oh where is last year's snow?

Where is the wise Eloise,
and Peter Abelard
gelded at Saint Denis
for love of her?
That queen who threw Buridan
in a sack in the Seine—
who will love her again?
Oh where is last year's snow?

Queen Blanche, the fleur-de-lys,
who had a siren's voice,
Bertha Big Foot, Beatrice,
Arembourg, ruler of Maine,
or Jeanne d'Arc of Lorraine
the British burned at Rouen?
Where are they, where? Oh Virgin,
where is last year's snow?

Prince, do not ask this year
or next year, where they are;
or answer my refrain:
Oh where is last year's snow?

Villon: *Le grand testament.*

The Old Lady's Lament for Her Youth

I think I heard the belle
we called the Armoress
lamenting her lost youth;
this was her whore's language:
"Oh treacherous, fierce old age,
you've gnawed me with your tooth,
yet if I end this mess
and die, I go to hell.

"You've stolen the great power
my beauty had on squire,
clerk, monk and general;
once there was no man born
who wouldn't give up all
(whatever his desire)
to have me for an hour—
this body beggars scorn!

"Once I broke the crown's laws,
and fled priests with a curse,
because I kept a boy,
and taught him what I knew—
alas, I only threw
myself away, because
I wanted to enjoy
this pimp, who loved my purse.

"I loved him when he hid
money, or used to bring
home whores and smash my teeth—
Oh when I lay beneath,
I forgave everything—
my tongue stuck to his tongue!
Tell me what good I did?
What's left? Disease and dung.

"He's dead these thirty years,
and I live on, grow old,
and think of that good time,
what was, what I've become;
sometimes, when I behold
my naked flesh, so numb,
dry, poor and small with time,
I cannot stop my tears.

"Where's my large Norman brow,
arched lashes, yellow hair,
the wide-eyed looks I used
to trap the cleverest men?
Where is my clear, soft skin,
neither too brown or fair,
my pointed ears, my bruised
red lips? I want to know.

"Where's the long neck I bent
swanlike, when asking pardon?
My small breasts, and the lips
of my vagina that sat
inside a little garden
and overlooked my hips,
plump, firm and so well set
for love's great tournament?

"Now wrinkled cheeks, and thin
wild lashes; nets of red
string fill the eyes that used
to look and laugh men dead.
How nature has abused
me. Wrinkles plow across
the brow, the lips are skin,
my ears hang down like moss.

"This is how beauty dies:
humped shoulders, barrenness
of mind; I've lost my hips,
vagina, and my lips.
My breasts? They're a retreat!
Short breath—how I repeat
my silly list! My thighs
are blotched like sausages.

"This is how we discuss
ourselves, and nurse desire
here as we gab about
the past, boneless as wool
dolls by a greenwood fire—
soon lit, and soon put out.
Once I was beautiful . . .
That's how it goes with us."

*   *   *

Villon: *Le grand testament.*

Villon's Prayer for His Mother to Say to the Virgin

Lastly I give the poor
woman, my mother, who bore
much pain for me—God knows!
this prayer to our Mistress,
Mary, my house and fortress
against the ills and sorrows
of life. I have no other
patron, nor has my mother.

"Lady of heaven, queen of the world,
and ruler of the underworld,
receive your humble Christian child,
and let him live with those you save;
although my soul is not much worth
saving, my Mistress and my Queen,
your grace is greater than my sin—
without you no man may deserve,
or enter heaven. I do not lie:
in this faith let me live and die.

"Say to your Son that I am his;
Mary of Egypt was absolved,
also the clerk, Theophilus,
whom you consented to restore,
although he'd made a pact with hell.
Save me from ever doing such ill,
our bond with evil is dissolved,
Oh Virgin, undefiled, who bore
Christ whom we celebrate at Mass—
in this faith let me live and die.

"I am a woman—poor, absurd,
who never learned to read your word—
at Mass each Sunday, I have seen
a painted paradise with lutes
and harps, a hell that boils the damned:
one gives me joy, the other doubts.
Oh let me have your joy, my Queen,
bountiful, honest and serene,
by whom no sinner is condemned—
in this faith let me live and die.

"You bore, oh Virgin and Princess,
Jesus, whose Kingdom never ends—
Our Lord took on our littleness,
and walked the world to save his friends—
he gave his lovely youth to death,
that's why I say to my last breath
in this faith let me live and die."

Villon: *Le grand testament.*

Villon's Epitaph

"Oh brothers, you live after us,
because we shared your revenue.
God may have mercy upon you,
if you have mercy upon us.
Five, six—you see us tied up here,
the flesh we overfed hangs here,
our carrion rots through skin and shirt,
and we, the bones, have changed to dirt.
Do not laugh at our misery:
pray God to save your souls and ours!

We hang in chains to satisfy
your justice and your violence,
brother humans—surely, you see
that all men cannot have good sense!
Here no man may look down on us—
Oh Child of Mary, pity us,
forgive our crimes—if dying well
saved even the poor thief from hell,
the blood of Christ will not run dry:
pray God to save your souls and ours!

The rain has soaked and washed us bare,
the sun has burned us black. Magpies
and crows have chiselled out our eyes,
have jerked away our beards and hair.
Our bodies have no time to rest:
our chains clank north, south, east and west,
now here, now there, to the winds' dance—
more beaks of birds than knives in France!
Do not join our fraternity:
pray God to save your souls and ours!

Prince Jesus, king of earth and air,
preserve our bodies from hell's powers—
we have no debts or business there.
We were not hanged to make you laugh.
Villon, who wrote our epitaph,
prays God to save your souls and ours!"

Villon: *Ballade des pendus.*

The Infinite

That hill pushed off by itself was always dear
to me and the hedges near
it that cut away so much of the final horizon.
When I would sit there lost in deliberation,
I reasoned most on the interminable spaces
beyond all hills, on their antediluvian resignation
and silence that passes
beyond man's possibility.
Here for a little while my heart is quiet inside me;
and when the wind lifts roughing through the trees,
I set about comparing my silence to those voices,
and I think about the eternal, the dead seasons,
things here at hand and alive,
and all their reasons and choices.
It's sweet to destroy my mind
and go down
and wreck in this sea where I drown.

Leopardi: *L'infinito.*

Saturday Night in the Village

The day
is ready to close;
the girl takes the downward
path homeward from the vineyard,
and jumps from crevice to crevice
like a goat, as she holds a swath
of violets and roses
to decorate her hair and bodice
tomorrow as usual for the Sabbath.

Her grandmother sits,
facing the sun going out,
and spins and starts to reason
with the neighbors, and renew the day,
when she used to dress herself for the holiday
and dance away
the nights—still quick and healthy,
with the boys, companions of her fairer season.

Once again the landscape is brown,
the sky drains to a pale blue,
shadows drop from mountain and thatch,
the young moon whitens.
As I catch
the clatter of small bells,
sounding in the holiday,

I can almost say
my heart takes comfort in the sound.
Children place their pickets
and sentinels,
and splash round and round
the village fountain.
They jump like crickets,
and make a happy sound.
The field-hand,
who lives on nothing,
marches home whistling,
and gorges on the day of idleness at hand.

Then all's at peace;
the lights are out;
I hear the rasp of shavings,
and the rapping hammer
of the carpenter, working all night
by lanternlight—
hurrying and straining himself
to increase his savings
before the whitening day.

This is the most kind
of the seven days; tomorrow, you will wait
and pray for Sunday's boredom and anguish
to be extinguished
in the workdays' grind
you anticipate.

Lively boy,
the only age you are alive
is like this day of joy,
a clear and breathless Saturday
that heralds life's holiday.
Rejoice, my child,
this is the untroubled instant.
Why should I undeceive you?
Let it not grieve you,
if the following day is slow to arrive.

Leopardi: *Il sabato del villaggio.*

Sylvia

Sylvia, do you remember the minutes
in this life overhung by death,
when beauty flamed
through your shy, serious meditations,
and you leapt beyond the limits
of girlhood?

Wild,
lightning-eyed child,
your incessant singing
shook the mirror-bright cobbles,
and even the parlor,
shuttered from summer,
where you sat at your sewing
and such girlish things—
happy enough to catch
at the future's blurred offer.
It was the great May,
and this is how you spent your day.

I could forget
the fascinating studies in my bolted room,
where my life was burning out,
and the heat
of my writings made the letters wriggle and melt
under drops of sweat.

Sometimes, I lolled on the railing of my father's house,
and pricked up my ears, and heard the noise
of your voice
and your hand run
to the hum of the monotonous loom.

I marvelled at the composed sky,
the little sun-guilded dust-paths,
and the gardens, running high
and half out of sight,
with the mountains on one side and the Adriatic
far off to the right.
How can human tongue
say what I felt?

What tremendous meaning, supposing,
and light-heartedness, my Sylvia!
What a Marie-Antoinette
stage-set
for life and its limits!
When I think of that great puff of pride,
sour constrictions choke me,
I turn aside to deride
my chances wrenched into misadventure.
Nature, harsh Nature,
why will you not pay
your promise today?
Why have you set
your children a bird-net?

Even before the Sirocco had sucked
the sap from the grass,
some undiagnosable disease
struck you and broke you—
you died, child,
and never saw your life flower,
or your flower plucked
by young men courting you
and arguing love
on the long Sunday walk—
their heads turned and lost
in your quick, shy talk.

Thus hope subsided
little by little;
fate decided
I was never to flower.
Hope, dear comrade of my shrinking summer,
how little you could keep
your color! You make me weep.
Is this your world?
These, its diversions, its infatuations,
its accomplishments, its sensations,
we used to unravel together?
You broke before the first
advance of truth;
the grave
was the final, shining milestone
you had always been pointing to
with such insistence
in the undistinguishable distance.

Leopardi: A Silvia.

Sic Transit

[*A conversation on the Basel road between
Steinen and Bromback, at night.*]

THE BOY

Now nearly always, Father, when I see
Rötteln Castle stand out like that, I wonder
if our own house will go down that way too.
Just look at it, it hangs there as tattered
and black as Death in the Dance of Death at Basel.
The more I look at it, the worse I feel.
Our house sits on a hill; it's like a church;
its leaded windows glitter; it looks grand.
Father, will our house tumble like the castle?
Sometimes, I think it simply must not happen.

FATHER

God help us, of course it must; what do you think?
Things start out young and new, and then they slide
gently downhill. They age and ache to their end;
nothing stands still. You hear the water rush?
You see how the stars hang side by side up there?
Perhaps you think things in the world stand still? No,
all's on the move, everything grows, then goes.

That's how things are; you mustn't stare at me.
You're young still, I was just as young once, now
I'm changed, and age, old age, is coming on,
and everywhere I go, to Wies, to Basel,
to the fields, woods, or home, it's all the same,
I'm travelling to the churchyard—that's the story;
when you are bearded, grown, and old as I,
I shan't be watching; sheep and goats will graze
over my grave. Our house is growing dirty;
night after night, the rain will wash it blacker,
day by day, the sun will blister away its trim;
you'll feel the raindrops thudding through its loft,
you'll hear the black winds whistling through its cracks,
the beetles click and tick behind its wainscot,
and when you die, my Son, your children's children
will come and patch it up, but then the rot
will ooze away its frame and underpinnings,
and when the year 2000 comes around,
all will be gone, our village will have slumped
into its grave. In time, the plough will go
where the church stood, the mayor's house and the rector's.

BOY
How silly, Father!

FATHER
                    No, stop staring at me;
that's how things are. Take Basel, it's a great
city with houses larger than most churches,
more churches than the houses in our village.
Basel! what is it? It's a crowd of people,
mountains of money, armies of gentlemen,

and there's another larger city, full
of men and women I knew once—they lie
behind the cloisters of the Munsterplatz,
and sleep. All's dead there, but the hour will strike,
when even Basel must fall down and die,
and only stick an arm up here and there:
a gable, a cellar, a tower, or a chimney,
an elm here, here a beech, or there a fir,
crab-grass and moss and ferns; herons will wade
through marshy basements—it is sad, my Son,
but there's no help, and ghosts will roister there,
if people are as silly then as now!
Frau Fast—she is already there, I think—
and Lippi Lappelli, God knows who besides . . .
Why do you push me with your elbow, Son?

BOY

Hush Father, wait until we've crossed the bridge,
and left that creepy wood and hill behind us.
A madman takes pot-shots at boys up there.
That clump there's where the girl who peddled eggs
died slashed and murdered, seven months ago.
Look how our Laubi* snorts and shies away!

FATHER

Son, don't be childish. Laubi has a cold.
The dead people hurt us much less than the living.
What was I saying? Oh yes, Basel. Basel
will go, and if some traveller passes by,
just half an hour or even an hour away,

* Laubi is one of the two oxen.

he'll stare across its dust, if there's no mist,
and say to his companion, "That was Basel;
that hump of litter was St. Peter's Church.
It's sad it's finished!"

BOY

                    Father, you are teasing.
What do you mean?

FATHER

                    That's how things are, my son,
stop staring at me like a child. In time,
the world and all its growth will change to fire;
then in the middle of the night, a watchman,
some foreigner that no one knows, will come.
He'll glitter like Napoleon's star, and shout:
"Wake up, wake up! The Day has come!" The sky
will redden, there'll be thunder everywhere,
first soft, then loud, like the French Terrorists'
bombardment here in seventeen-ninety-six.
The earth will totter, and make the churches rock,
they'll toll their bells for service far and wide,
and everyone will pray. The Day will come;
oh God preserve us, we won't need the sun then,
the heavens will be a waterfall of lightning,
and earth a hod of coals. Lots more will happen.
I have no time to tell you; everything
will catch and burn wherever there is land.
No one will be anywhere to put it out;
it'll have to put itself out in the end.
What do you think the earth will look like then?

BOY

Don't tell me, Father! What will happen to all
the people, when everything is burned and burning?

FATHER

When the fire comes, the people won't be there,
they'll be . . . where will they be? Live right, do good
whatever happens, keep a pure conscience.
Do you see how the sky streams with bright stars?
Each star might be a village; farther up,
perhaps, there is a capital. Go easy,
it can't be seen from here. Live right, do good,
and you will go to one of those bright stars;
I'll be there, if God's willing, and your mother,
my poor Elizabeth. Perhaps, you'll drive
a pair of oxen up the Milky Way,
and find the unknown city—looking down
from one side earthward then, what will you see?
Rötteln Castle! The Belchen will be charred,
and the Blauen . . . just like two old chimneys,
and everything between them will have burned
down to the ground. There won't be any water
then in the Wiese, everything will be
gritty and black and still as death itself,
as far as eye can reach. You'll see all that,
and say to your companion, "Take a look!
That's where the world was, that black mountain, that
was called the Belchen, over there is Wieslet—
I lived there once, and used to harness oxen
to carry mountain-loads of oak to Basel,

there's where I plowed and drained the bottom land,
scared rabbits through the brush, made splints for torches . . .
That's where I learned to drudge away my life.
All the king's horses cannot drag me back!"

Hebel: *Die Vergänglichkeit.*

Heine Dying in Paris

I

DEATH AND MORPHINE

Yes, in the end they are much of a pair,
my twin gladiator beauties—thinner than a hair,
their bronze bell-heads hum with the void; one's more austere,
however, and much whiter; none dares cry down his character.
How confidingly the corrupt twin rocked me in his arms;
his poppy garland, nearing, hushed death's alarms
at sword-point for a moment.
Soon a pinpoint of infinite regression! And now that incident
is closed. There's no way out,
unless the other turn about
and, pale, distinguished, perfect, drop his torch.
He and I stand alerted for life's Doric, drilled, withdrawing march:
sleep is lovely, death is better still,
not to have been born is of course the miracle.

II

Every idle desire has died in my breast;
even hatred of evil things, even my feeling
for my own and other men's distress.
What lives in me is death.
The curtain falls, the play is done;
my dear German public is goosestepping home, yawning.
They are no fools, these good people:
they are slurping their dinners quite happily,
bear-hugging beer-mugs—singing and laughing.

That fellow in Homer's book was quite right:
he said: the meanest little Philistine living
in Stukkert-am-Neckar is luckier
than I, the golden-haired Achilles, the dead lion,
glorious shadow-king of the underworld.

III

My zenith was luckily happier than my night:
whenever I touched the lyre of inspiration, I smote
the Chosen People. Often—all sex and thunder—
I pierced those overblown and summer clouds . . .
But my summer has flowered. My sword is scabbarded
in the marrow of my spinal discs.
Soon I must lose all these half-gods
that made my world so agonizingly half-joyful.

The hand clangs to a close on the dominant;
the champagne glass of orange sherbet breaks
on my lips—all glass; straws in the wind?
Little Aristophanes? I give my sugared leasehold on life
to the great Aristophanes and author of life—
midsummer's frail and green-juice bird's-nest.

Heine: *Morphine; Der Scheidende; Mein Tag war heiter*.

Russia 1812

The snow fell, and its power was multiplied.
For the first time the Eagle bowed its head—
dark days! Slowly the Emperor returned—
behind him Moscow! Its onion domes still burned.
The snow rained down in blizzards—rained and froze.
Past each white waste a further white waste rose.
None recognized the captains or the flags.
Yesterday the Grand Army, today its dregs!
No one could tell the vanguard from the flanks.
The snow! The hurt men struggled from the ranks,
hid in the bellies of dead horse, in stacks
of shattered caissons. By the bivouacs,
one saw the picket dying at his post,
still standing in his saddle, white with frost,
the stone lips frozen to the bugle's mouth!
Bullets and grapeshot mingled with the snow,
that hailed . . . The Guard, surprised at shivering, march
in a dream now; ice rimes the gray mustache.
The snow falls, always snow! The driving mire
submerges; men, trapped in that white empire,
have no more bread and march on barefoot—gaps!
They were no longer living men and troops,
but a dream drifting in a fog, a mystery,
mourners parading under the black sky.
The solitude, vast, terrible to the eye,
was like a mute avenger everywhere,

as snowfall, floating through the quiet air,
buried the huge army in a huge shroud.
Could anyone leave this kingdom? A crowd—
each man, obsessed with dying, was alone.
Men slept—and died! The beaten mob sludged on,
ditching the guns to burn their carriages.
Two foes. The North, the Czar. The North was worse.
In hollows where the snow was piling up,
one saw whole regiments fallen asleep.
Attila's dawn, Cannaes of Hannibal!
The army marching to its funeral!
Litters, wounded, the dead, deserters—swarm,
crushing the bridges down to cross a stream.
They went to sleep ten thousand, woke up four.
Ney, bringing up the former army's rear,
hacked his horse loose from three disputing Cossacks . . .
All night, the *qui vive?* The alert! Attacks;
retreats! White ghosts would wrench away our guns,
or we would see dim, terrible squadrons,
circles of steel, whirlpools of savages,
rush sabering through the camp like dervishes.
And in this way, whole armies died at night.

The Emperor was there, standing—he saw.
This oak already trembling from the axe,
watched his glories drop from him branch by branch:
chiefs, soldiers. Each one had his turn and chance—
they died! Some lived. These still believed his star,
and kept their watch. They loved the man of war,
this small man with his hands behind his back,
whose shadow, moving to and fro, was black
behind the lighted tent. Still believing, they

accused their destiny of *lese-majesté*.
His misfortune had mounted on their back.
The man of glory shook. Cold stupefied
him, then suddenly he felt terrified.
Being without belief, he turned to God:
"God of armies, is this the end?" he cried.
And then at last the expiation came,
as he heard some one call him by his name,
some one half-lost in shadow, who said, "No,
Napoleon." Napoleon understood,
restless, bareheaded, leaden, as he stood
before his butchered legions in the snow.

Victor Hugo: *L'expiation*.

At Gautier's Grave

Friend, poet, spirit—you have fled our night,
and leave its dark to voyage for the light;
here on the tomb's severe sill, I greet you:
you knew the beautiful, go, find the true!
Somewhere you shine, and I who knew you young
and gallant, I who loved you, I who hung
on your supporting shoulder, when I fled,
broken, from the great flights: I'm seventy, white
with the old years that snow down on my head,
I think of the bright times that changed to worse,
that young past, when we saw the rising day,
the fight, the tumult, the arena curse
and cheer our new art offered to the mob.

Yes, I listen: the great wind dies away,
I feel the summit's sinister cold breath,
I hurry. Do not close the gate of death,
for when my friends die, I start back and see
their fixed eyes draw me to infinity;
I have begun to die by being alone,
I banished here, I who must soon be gone;
my night is breaking vaguely into stars,
my too long thread thrills, quivers for the shears!

We die. That is the law. None holds it back,
all leans; and this great age with all its light
glides to the shadow, where we flee—pale, black!
The oaks felled for the pyre of Hercules,
what a harsh roar they make in the red night!
Death's horses throw their heads, neigh, roll their eyes—
they are joyful, for the shining day now dies,
our age that mastered the high wind and wave
expires . . . And you, their brother and their peer,
join Lamartine, Dumas, Musset—Gautier,
the ancient sea that made us young is dry,
youth has no fountain, age has no more Styx,
and Time moves forward with his heavy blade,
thoughtful, and step by step, to the last ear.
My turn comes round; night fills my troubled eye,
which prophesies the future from the past,
weeps over cribs, and smiles at this new grave.

Victor Hugo: *A Théophile Gautier.*

To the Reader

(For Stanley Kunitz)

Infatuation, sadism, lust, avarice
possess our souls and drain the body's force;
we spoonfeed our adorable remorse,
like whores or beggars nourishing their lice.

Our sins are mulish, our confessions lies;
we play to the grandstand with our promises,
we pray for tears to wash our filthiness,
importantly pissing hogwash through our styes.

The devil, watching by our sickbeds, hissed
old smut and folk-songs to our soul, until
the soft and precious metal of our will
boiled off in vapor for this scientist.

Each day his flattery makes us eat a toad,
and each step forward is a step to hell,
unmoved, though previous corpses and their smell
asphyxiate our progress on this road.

Like the poor lush who cannot satisfy,
we try to force our sex with counterfeits,
die drooling on the deliquescent tits,
mouthing the rotten orange we suck dry.

Gangs of demons are boozing in our brain—
ranked, swarming, like a million warrior-ants,
they drown and choke the cistern of our wants;
each time we breathe, we tear our lungs with pain.

If poison, arson, sex, narcotics, knives
have not yet ruined us and stitched their quick,
loud patterns on the canvas of our lives,
it is because our souls are still too sick.

Among the vermin, jackals, panthers, lice,
gorillas and tarantulas that suck
and snatch and scratch and defecate and fuck
in the disorderly circus of our vice,

there's one more ugly and abortive birth.
It makes no gestures, never beats its breast,
yet it would murder for a moment's rest,
and willingly annihilate the earth.

It's BOREDOM. Tears have glued its eyes together.
You know it well, my Reader. This obscene
beast chain-smokes yawning for the guillotine—
you—hypocrite Reader—my double—my brother!

Baudelaire: *Au lecteur.*

My Beatrice

While I was walking in a pitted place,
crying aloud against the human race,
letting thoughts ramble here and there apart—
knives singing on the whetstone of my heart—
I saw a cloud descending on my head
in the full noon, a cloud inhabited
by black devils, sharp, humped, inquisitive
as dwarfs. They knew where I was sensitive,
now idling there, and looked me up and down,
as cool delinquents watch a madman clown.
I heard them laugh and snicker blasphemies,
while swapping signs and blinking with their eyes.

"Let's stop and watch this creature at our leisure—
all sighs and sweaty hair. We'll take his measure.
It's a great pity that this mountebank
and ghost of Hamlet strutting on his plank
should think he's such an artist at his role
he has to rip the lining from his soul
and paralyze the butterflies and bees
with a peepshow of his indecencies—
and even we, who gave him his education,
must listen to his schoolboy declamation."

Wishing to play a part (my pride was high
above the mountains and the devil's cry)
like Hamlet now, I would have turned my back,
had I not seen among the filthy pack
(Oh crime that should have made the sun drop dead!)
my heart's queen and the mistress of my bed
there purring with the rest at my distress,
and sometimes tossing them a stale caress.

Baudelaire: *La Béatrice.*

Spleen

I'm like the king of a rain-country, rich
but sterile, young but with an old wolf's itch,
one who escapes Fénelon's apologues,
and kills the day in boredom with his dogs;
nothing cheers him, darts, tennis, falconry,
his people dying by the balcony;
the bawdry of the pet hermaphrodite
no longer gets him through a single night;
his bed of fleur-de-lys becomes a tomb;
even the ladies of the court, for whom
all kings are beautiful, cannot put on
shameful enough dresses for this skeleton;
the scholar who makes his gold cannot invent
washes to cleanse the poisoned element;
even in baths of blood, Rome's legacy,
our tyrants' solace in senility,
he cannot warm up his shot corpse, whose food
is syrup-green Lethean ooze, not blood.

Baudelaire: *Spleen.*

Autumn

Now colder shadows . . . Who'll turn back the clock?
Goodbye bright summer's brief too lively sport!
The squirrel drops its acorn with a shock,
cord-wood reverberates in my cobbled court.

Winter has entered in my citadel:
hate, anger, fear, forced work like splitting rock,
and like the sun borne to its northern hell,
my heart's no more than a red, frozen block.

Shaking, I listen for the wood to fall;
building a scaffold makes no deafer sound.
Each heart-beat knocks my body to the ground,
like a slow battering ram crumbling a wall.

I think this is the season's funeral,
some one is nailing a coffin hurriedly.
For whom? Yesterday summer, today fall—
the steady progress sounds like a goodbye.

Baudelaire: *Chant d'automne.*

The Ruined Garden

My childhood was only a menacing shower,
cut now and then by hours of brilliant heat.
All the top soil was killed by rain and sleet,
my garden hardly bore a standing flower.

From now on, my mind's autumn! I must take
the field and dress my beds with spade and rake
and restore order to my flooded grounds.
There the rain raised mountains like burial mounds.

I throw fresh seeds out. Who knows what survives?
What elements will give us life and food?
This soil is irrigated by the tides.

Time and nature sluice away our lives.
A virus eats the heart out of our sides,
digs in and multiplies on our lost blood.

Baudelaire: *L'ennemi.*

The Flawed Bell

Propped on my footstool by the popping log
and sitting out the winter night, I hear
my boyish falsetto crack and disappear
to the sound of the bells jangling through the fog.

Lucky the carrying and loud-tongued bell,
whose metal fights the wear and rust of time
to piously repeat its fractured chime,
like an old trooper playing sentinel!

My soul is flawed, and often when I try
to shrug away my early decrepitude,
and populate the night with my shrill cry,

I hear the death-cough of mortality
choked under corpses by a lake of blood—
my rocklike, unhinging effort to die.

Baudelaire: *La cloche fêlée.*

Meditation

Calm down, my Sorrow, we must move with care.
You called for evening; it descends; it's here.
The town is coffined in its atmosphere,
bringing relief to some, to others care.

Now while the common multitude strips bare,
feels pleasure's cat o' nine tails on its back,
and fights off anguish at the great bazaar,
give me your hand, my Sorrow. Let's stand back;

back from these people! Look, the dead years dressed
in old clothes crowd the balconies of the sky.
Regret emerges smiling from the sea,

the sick sun slumbers underneath an arch,
and like a shroud strung out from east to west,
listen, my Dearest, hear the sweet night march!

Baudelaire: Recueillement.

The Injured Moon

Oh Moon, discreetly worshipped by our sires,
still riding through your high blue countries, still
trailed by the shining harem of your stars,
old Cynthia, the lamp of our retreats . . .

the lovers sleep open-mouthed! When they breathe,
they show the white enamel of their teeth.
The writer breaks his teeth on his work-sheets,
the vipers couple under the hot hill.

Dressed in your yellow hood, do you pursue
your boy from night to dawn, till the sun climbs
skyward, where dim Endymion disappears?

"I see your mother, Child of these poor times,
crushed to her mirror by the heavy years.
She cunningly powders the breast that nourished you."

Baudelaire: *La lune offensée.*

The Abyss

Pascal's abyss went with him at his side,
closer than blood—alas, activity,
dreams, words, desire: all holes! On every side,
spaces, the bat-wing of insanity!
Above, below me, only depths and shoal,
the silence! And the Lord's right arm
traces his nightmare, truceless, multiform.
I cuddle the insensible blank air,
and fear to sleep as one fears a great hole.
My spirit, haunted by its vertigo,
sees the infinite at every window,
vague, horrible, and dropping God knows where . . .
Ah never to escape from numbers and form!

Baudelaire: *Le gouffre.*

The Swan

Andromache, I think of you. Here men
move on, diminished, from those grander years,
when Racine's tirades scourged our greasy Seine,
this lying trickle swollen with your tears!

Some echo fertilized my magpie mind,
as I was crossing the new Carrousel.
Old Paris is done for. (Our cities find
new faces sooner than the heart.) Its shell

was all I noticed, when I strolled beneath
its barracks, heaps of roughed-out capitals,
stray apple carts, troughs, greening horses' teeth,
commercial gypsies clinking in their stalls.

A strolling circus had laid out its tent,
where I was dragging home through the dawn's red;
labor was rising, and a sprinkler spread
a hurricane to lay the sediment.

I saw a swan that had escaped its cage,
and struck its dry wings on the cobbled street,
and drenched the curbing with its fluffy plumage.
Beside a gritty gutter, it dabbed its feet,

and gobbled at the dust to stop its thirst.
Its heart was full of its blue lakes, and screamed:
"Water, when will you fall? When will you burst,
oh thunderclouds?" How often I have dreamed

I see this bird like Ovid exiled here
in Paris, its Black Sea—it spears and prods
its snake-head at our blue, ironic air,
as if it wanted to reproach the gods.

II

Paris changes; nothing in my melancholy
stirs . . . new mansards, *arrondisements* razed *en bloc,*
glass, scaffolding, slum wards—all allegory!
My memories are heavier than rock!

Here by the Louvre my symbol oppresses me:
I think of the great swan hurled from the blue,
heroic, silly—like a refugee
dogged by its griping angst—also of you,

Andromache, fallen from your great bridegroom,
and now the concubine and baggage of Pyrrhus—
you loiter wailing by the empty tomb,
Hector's widow and the last wife of Helenus!

I think of you, tubercular and sick,
blindly stamping through puddles, Jeanne Duval,
peering into the Paris fog's thick wall
for the lost coco-palms of Mozambique.

I think of people who have lost the luck
they never find again, and waste their powers,
like wolf-nurses giving grief a tit to suck,
or public orphans drying up like flowers;

and in this forest, on my downward drag,
my old sorrow lets out its lion's roar.
I think of Paris raising the white flag,
drowned sailors, fallen girls . . . and many more!

Baudelaire: Le cygne.

Voyage to Cythera

My heart, a seagull rocketed and spun
about the rigging, dipping joyfully;
our slow prow rocking under cloudless sky
was like an angel drunk with the live sun.

What's that out there? Those leagues of hovering sand?
"It's Cythera famous in the songs,
the gay old dogs' El Dorado, it belongs
to legend. Look closely, it's a poor land."

Island of secret orgies none profess,
the august shade of Aphrodite plays
like clouds of incense over your blue bays,
and weights the heart with love and weariness.

Island whose myrtle esplanades arouse
our nerves, here heart-sighs and the adoration
of every land and age and generation
ramble like coal-red roses on a house

to the eternal cooing of the dove.
"No, Cythera crumbles, cakes and dries,
a rocky desert troubled by shrill cries . . .
And yet I see one portent stretch above

us. Is it a temple where the pagan powers
hover in naked majesty to bless
the arbors, gold-fish ponds and terraces;
and the young priestess is in love with flowers?

No, nosing through these shoals, and coming near
enough to scare the birds with our white sails,
we saw a man spread-eagled on the nails
of a cross hanging like a cypress there.

Ferocious vultures choking down thick blood
gutted the hanging man, already foul;
each smacked its beak like the flat of a trowel
into the private places of their food.

His eyes were holes and his important paunch
oozed lazy, looping innards down his hips;
those scavengers, licking sweetmeats from their lips,
had hung his pouch and penis on a branch.

Under his foot-soles, shoals of quadrupeds
with lifted muzzles nosed him round and guzzled;
a huge ante-diluvian reptile muscled
through them like an executioner with his aides.

Native of Cythera, initiate,
how silently you hung and suffered insult
in retribution for your dirty cult
and orgasms only death could expiate.

Ridiculous hanged man, my sins confirm
your desecration; when I saw you seethe,
I felt my nausea mounting to my teeth,
the drying bile-stream of my wasted sperm.

Poor devil with sweet memories, your laws
are mine; before you, I too felt those jaws:
black panther, lancing crow, the Noah's Ark
that loved to chafe my flesh and leave their mark.

I'd lost my vision clinging to those shrouds,
I feared the matching blues of sky and sea;
all things were henceforth black with blood for me,
and plunged my heart in allegoric clouds . . .

Nothing stands upright in your land, oh Lust,
except my double, hanging at full length—
Oh God, give me the courage and the strength
to see my heart and body without disgust.

Baudelaire: *Voyage à Cythère.*

The Servant

My old nurse and servant, whose great heart
made you jealous, is dead and sleeps apart
from us. Shouldn't we bring her a few flowers?
The dead, the poor dead, they have their bad hours,
and when October stripper of old trees,
poisons the turf and makes their marble freeze,
surely they find us worse than wolves or curs
for sleeping under mountainous warm furs . . .
These, eaten by the earth's black dream, lie dead,
without a wife or friend to warm their bed,
old skeletons sunk like shrubs in burlap bags—
and feel the ages trickle through their rags.
They have no heirs or relatives to chase
with children round their crosses and replace
the potted refuse, where they lie beneath
their final flower, the interment wreath.

The oak log sings and sputters in my chamber,
and in the cold blue half-light of December,
I see her tiptoe through my room, and halt
humbly, as if she'd hurried from her vault
with blankets for the child her sleepless eye
had coaxed and mothered to maturity.
What can I say to her to calm her fears?
My nurse's hollow sockets fill with tears.

Baudelaire: *La servante*

The Game

Cheeks chalked, blacked lashes, eyes still terrible—
old bags glittering under chandeliers,
as they titter and make a waterfall
of stone and metal fall from their thin ears;

my hang-dog shadow joining in the queue,
as fixtures holding fifty candles light
the profiles of great men who used to write,
and here gasp out their ulcerous guts to screw;

crowding this gameboard, faces without lips,
lips white as teeth, false uppers without jaws,
bone fingers running through the youthful grips,
still fumbling empty pockets and false bras . . .

This is the sort of tableau of my doom
self-love imagines for my terminus;
stuck in a corner of the waiting-room,
I see myself withdrawn and lecherous—

envying the war-horses' running sores,
this one's torn nerves, that one's arthritic grace,
the graveyard gaiety of these old whores,
angling their flesh for traffic in my face—

envying those who scuttle character,
and crowd full sail into the blue abyss—
these drunk for blood, who in the end prefer
dishonor to death, and hell to nothingness.

Baudelaire: *Le jeu*

The Voyage

(*For T. S. Eliot*)

I

For the boy playing with his globe and stamps,
the world is equal to his appetite—
how grand the world in the blaze of the lamps,
how petty in tomorrow's small dry light!

One morning we lift anchor, full of brave
prejudices, prospects, ingenuity—
we swing with the velvet swell of the wave,
our infinite is rocked by the fixed sea.

Some wish to fly a cheapness they detest,
others, their cradles' terror—others stand
with their binoculars on a woman's breast,
reptilian Circe with her junk and wand.

Not to be turned to reptiles, such men daze
themselves with spaces, light, the burning sky;
cold toughens them, they bronze in the sun's blaze
and dry the sores of their debauchery.

But the true voyagers are those who move
simply to move—like lost balloons! Their heart
is some old motor thudding in one groove.
It says its single phrase, "Let us depart!"

They are like conscripts lusting for the guns;
our sciences have never learned to tag
their projects and designs—enormous, vague
hopes grease the wheels of these automatons!

II

We imitate, oh horror! tops and bowls
in their eternal waltzing marathon;
even in sleep, our fever whips and rolls—
like a black angel flogging the brute sun.

Strange sport! where destination has no place
or name, and may be anywhere we choose—
where man, committed to his endless race,
runs like a madman diving for repose!

Our soul is a three-master seeking port:
a voice from starboard shouts, "We're at the dock!"
Another, more elated, cries from port,
"Here's dancing, gin and girls!" Balls! it's a rock!

The islands sighted by the lookout seem
the El Dorados promised us last night;
imagination wakes from its drugged dream,
sees only ledges in the morning light.

What dragged these patients from their German spas?
Shall we throw them in chains, or in the sea?
Sailors discovering new Americas,
who drown in a mirage of agony!

The worn-out sponge, who scuffles through our slums
sees whiskey, paradise and liberty
wherever oil-lamps shine in furnished rooms—
we see Blue Grottoes, Caesar and Capri.

III

Stunningly simple Tourists, your pursuit
is written in the tear-drops in your eyes!
Spread out the packing cases of your loot,
your azure sapphires made of seas and skies!

We want to break the boredom of our jails
and cross the oceans without oars or steam—
give us visions to stretch our minds like sails,
the blue, exotic shoreline of your dream!

Tell us, what have you seen?

IV

                "We've seen the stars,
a wave or two—we've also seen some sand;
although we peer through telescopes and spars,
we're often deadly bored as you on land.

The shine of sunlight on the violet sea,
the roar of cities when the sun goes down:
these stir our hearts with restless energy;
we worship the Indian Ocean where we drown!

No old chateau or shrine besieged by crowds
of crippled pilgrims sets our souls on fire,
as these chance countries gathered from the clouds.
Our hearts are always anxious with desire.

Desire, that great elm fertilized by lust,
gives its old body, when the heaven warms
its bark that winters and old age encrust;
green branches draw the sun into its arms.

Why are you always growing taller, Tree—
Oh longer-lived than cypress! Yet we took
one or two sketches for your picture-book,
Brothers who sell your souls for novelty!

We have salaamed to pagan gods with horns,
entered shrines peopled by a galaxy
of Buddhas, Slavic saints, and unicorns,
so rich Rothschild must dream of bankruptcy!

Priests' robes that scattered solid golden flakes,
dancers with tatooed bellies and behinds,
charmers supported by braziers of snakes . . ."

V

Yes, and what else?

VI

Oh trivial, childish minds!

You've missed the more important things that we
were forced to learn against our will. We've been
from top to bottom of the ladder, and see
only the pageant of immortal sin:

there women, servile, peacock-tailed, and coarse,
marry for money, and love without disgust
horny, pot-bellied tyrants stuffed on lust,
slaves' slaves—the sewer in which their gutter pours!

old maids who weep, playboys who live each hour,
state banquets loaded with hot sauces, blood and trash,
ministers sterilized by dreams of power,
workers who love their brutalizing lash;

and everywhere religions like our own
all storming heaven, propped by saints who reign
like sybarites on beds of nails and frown—
all searching for some orgiastic pain!

70

Many, self-drunk, are lying in the mud—
mad now, as they have always been, they roll
in torment screaming to the throne of God:
"My image and my lord, I hate your soul!"

And others, dedicated without hope,
flee the dull herd—each locked in his own world
hides in his ivory-tower of art and dope—
this is the daily news from the whole world!

VII

How sour the knowledge travellers bring away!
The world's monotonous and small; we see
ourselves today, tomorrow, yesterday,
an oasis of horror in sands of ennui!

Shall we move or rest? Rest, if you can rest;
move if you must. One runs, but others drop
and trick their vigilant antagonist.
Time is a runner who can never stop,

the Wandering Jew or Christ's Apostles. Yet
nothing's enough; no knife goes through the ribs
of this retarius throwing out his net;
others can kill and never leave their cribs.

And even when Time's heel is on our throat
we still can hope, still cry, "On, on, let's go!"
Just as we once took passage on the boat
for China, shivering as we felt the blow,

so we now set our sails for the Dead Sea,
light-hearted as the youngest voyager.
If you look seaward, Traveller, you will see
a spectre rise and hear it sing, "Stop, here,

and eat my lotus-flowers, here's where they're sold.
Here are the fabulous fruits; look, my boughs bend;
eat yourself sick on knowledge. Here we hold
time in our hands, it never has to end."

We know the accents of this ghost by heart;
Our comrade spreads his arms across the seas;
"On, on, Orestes. Sail and feast your heart—
Here's Clytemnestra." Once we kissed her knees.

VIII

It's time. Old Captain, Death, lift anchor, sink!
The land rots; we shall sail into the night;
if now the sky and sea are black as ink,
our hearts, as you must know, are filled with light.

Only when we drink poison are we well—
we want, this fire so burns our brain tissue,
to drown in the abyss—heaven or hell,
who cares? Through the unknown, we'll find the *new*.

Baudelaire: *Le voyage.*

Nostalgia

[*An autobiographical poem: Rimbaud remembers the small boy in a rowboat under the old walls of Charleville. His mother and sisters are on the bank. His father has just deserted them.*]

I

The sucking river was the child's salt tears.
His eyes were blinded by white walls; the girls,
white lilies on white silk! The *Tricouleur*
hung from the walls restored by Joan of Arc—

wings of an angel! No, the gold stream slid,
breathing the underwater amber of its reeds . . .
His mother had the blue sky for parasol,
yet begged the arched bridge and the hills for shade.

II

Then the walled surface swam with bubbles;
cloth of gold coverings piled the riverbed;
the sisters' faded grass-bruised pinafores
hung like willows; birds stepped from twig to twig.

Through noon, the river's spotted mirror steamed
off to the bare sky's perfect, burning sphere—
Oh Bride, your faith was purer than gold coins,
marsh marigolds, my hot and burning eyelid . . .

III

The mother stood too stiffly in the field,
beclouded with the field-hands' shirts. She twirled
her parasol, and trampled on the weeds.
The sisters sat on the heraldic green,

and stared at red Morocco Missals, while
his father walked beyond the mountain, like
a thousand angels parting on the road.
She, cold and black, flew. Rushed after her lost man!

IV

Nostalgia for his hairy arms—the grass
green in the holy April moonlight! Joy!
The riverbank's abandoned lumberyards
still fertilized the marsh with blocks and sawdust.

She wept below the parapet. The breath
of the dry poplars was the wind's alone;
the water had no bottom and no source;
a man in mud-caked hip-boots poled a barge.

V

The dull eye drove the water out of reach—
still boat, oh too short arms! I could not touch
one or the other flower—the yellow burned me,
the cool blue was the ash-gray water's friend.

The reeds had eaten up the roses long ago;
each wing-beat shook the willows' silver dust.
My boat stuck fast; its anchor dug for bottom;
the lidless eye, still water, filled with mud.

Rimbaud: *Mémoire*.

The Poet at Seven

When the timeless, daily, tedious affair
was over, his Mother shut
her Bible; her nose was in the air;
from her summit
of righteousness, she could not see the boy:
his lumpy forehead knotted
with turmoil, his soul returned to its vomit.

All day he would sweat obedience.
He was very intelligent, but wrung,
and every now and then a sudden jerk
showed dark hypocrisies at work.
He would clap his hands on his rump,
and strut where the gloom of the hallway rotted
the hot curtains. He stuck out his tongue,
clenched his eyes shut, and saw dots.
A terrace gave on the twilight;
one used to see him up there in the lamplight,
sulking on the railing
under an abyss of air
which hung from the roof. His worst block
was the stultifying slump
of mid-summer—he would lock
himself up in the toilet and inhale
its freshness; there he could breathe.

When winter snowed under the breath of flowers,
and the moon blanched the little bower
behind the house, he would crawl
to the foot of the wall
and lie with his eyeballs squeezed to his arm,
dreaming of some dark revelation,
or listening to the legions of termites swarm
in the horny espaliers. As for compassion,
the only children he could speak to
were creepy, abstracted boys, who hid
match-stick thin fingers yellow and black with mud
under rags stuck with diarrhea.
Their dull eyes drooled on their dull cheeks,
they spoke with the selflessness of morons.
His Mother was terrified,
she thought they were losing caste. This was good—
she had the true blue look that lied.

At seven he was making novels
about life in the Sahara,
where ravished Liberty had fled—
sunrises, buffaloes, jungle, savannahs!
For his facts, he used illustrated weeklies,
and blushed at the rotogravures of naked, red
Hawaiian girls dancing.
A little eight year old tomboy,
the daughter of the next door workers,
came, brown-eyed, terrible,
·in a print dress. Brutal and in the know,
she would jump on his back,
and ride him like a buffalo,
and shake out her hair.

Wallowing below
her once, he bit her crotch—
she never wore bloomers—
kicked and scratched, he carried back
the taste of her buttocks to his bedroom.

What he feared most
were the sticky, lost December Sundays,
when he used to stand with his hair gummed back
at a little mahogony stand, and hold
a Bible pocked with cabbage-green mould.
Each night in his alcove, he had dreams.
He despised God, the National Guard,
and the triple drum-beat
of the town-crier calling up the conscripts.
He loved the swearing
workers, when they crowded back, black
in the theatrical twilight to their wards.
He felt clean
when he filled his lungs with the smell—
half hay fever, half iodine—
of the wheat,
he watched its pubic golden tassels swell
and steam in the heat,
then sink back calm.

What he liked best were dark things:
the acrid, dank rings
on the ceiling, and the high,
bluish plaster, as bald as the sky
in his bare bedroom, where he could close
the shutters and lose

79

his world for hundreds of hours,
mooning doggedly
over his novel, endlessly
expanding with jaundiced skies,
drowned vegetation, and carnations
that flashed like raw flesh
in the underwater green
of the jungle starred with flowers—
dizziness, mania, revulsions, pity!
Often the town playground
below him grew loud with children;
the wind brought him their voices,
and he lay alone on pieces of unbleached canvas,
violently breaking into sail.

Rimbaud: *Les poètes de sept ans.*

The Drunken Boat

I felt my guides no longer carried me—
as we sailed down the virgin Amazon,
the redskins nailed them to their painted stakes
naked, as targets for their archery.

I carried Flemish wheat or Swedish wood,
but had forgotten my unruly crew;
their conversation ended with their lives,
the river let me wander where I would.

Surf punished me, and threw my cargo out;
last winter I was breaking up on land.
I fled. These floating river villages
had never heard a more triumphant shout.

The green ooze spurting through my centerboard
was sweeter than sour apples to a boy—
it washed away the stains of puke and rot-gut,
anchor and wheel were carried overboard.

The typhoon spun my silly needle round;
ten nights I scudded from the freighters' lights;
lighter than cork, I danced upon the surge
man calls the rolling coffin of his drowned.

Rudderless, I was driven like a plank
on night seas stuck with stars and dribbling milk;
I shot through greens and blues, where luminous,
swollen, drowned sailors rose for light and sank.

I saw the lightning turn the pole-star green,
currents, icebergs, and waterspouts. One night
the sunrise lifted like a flock of doves—
I saw whatever men suppose they've seen.

I saw the ocean bellowing on the land,
cattle stampeding with their tails on fire,
but never dreamed Three Marys walked the sea
to curb those frothing muzzles with a hand.

I saw the salt marsh boil, a whole whale rot
in some Louisiana bayou's muck,
cutting the blue horizon with its flukes—
bon-bons of sunlight and cold azure snot!

I was a lost boat nosing through the hulls
of Monitors and Hanseatic hulks;
none cared to gaff my wreckage from the bilge
and yellow beaks of the marauding gulls.

I would have liked to show a child those seas,
rocking to soothe the clatter of my sails
in irons on the equatorial line.
Like a woman, I fell upon my knees;

then heaven opened for the voyager.
I stared at archipelagoes of stars.
Was it on those dead watches that I died—
a million golden birds, Oh future Vigor!

I cannot watch these purple suns go down
like actors on the Aeschylean stage.
I'm drunk on water. I cry out too much—
Oh that my keel might break, and I might drown!

Shrunken and black against a twilight sky,
our Europe has no water. Only a pond
the cows have left, and a boy wades to launch
his paper boat frail as a butterfly.

Bathed in your languors, Waves, I have no wings
to cut across the wakes of cotton ships,
or fly against the flags of merchant kings,
or swim beneath the guns of prison ships.

Rimbaud: *Bateau ivre.*

Eighteen-Seventy

I

A POSTER OF OUR DAZZLING VICTORY
AT SAARBRUCKEN

In the center of the poster, Napoleon
rides in apotheosis, sallow, medalled, a ramrod
perched on a merrygoround horse. He sees life
through rosy glasses, terrible as God,

and sentimental as a bourgeois papa.
Four little conscripts take their nap below
on scarlet guns and drums. One, unbuckling, cheers
Napoleon—he's stunned by the big name!

Another lounges on the butt of his Chassepot,
another feels his hair rise on his neck.
A bearskin shako bounds like a black sun:

VIVE L'EMPEREUR! They're holding back their breath.
And last, some moron, struggling to his knees,
presents a blue and scarlet ass—to what?

NAPOLEON AFTER SEDAN

The man waxy—he jogs along the fields
in flower, black, a cigar between his teeth.
The wax man thinks about the Tuilleries
in flower. At times his mossy eye takes fire.

Twenty years of orgy have made him drunk:
he'd said: "My hand will snuff out Liberty,
politely, gently, as I snuff my stogie."
Liberty lives; the Emperor is out—

he's captured. Oh what name is shaking on
his lips? What plebescites? Napoleon
cannot tell you. His shark's eye is dead.

An opera glass on the horses at Compere . . .
he watches his cigar fume off in smoke . . .
soirees at Saint Cloud . . . a bluish vapor.

III

TO THE FRENCH OF THE SECOND EMPIRE

You, dead in '92 and '93,
still pale from the great kiss of Liberty—
when tyrants trampled on humanity,
you broke them underneath your wooden shoes.

You were reborn and great by agony,
your hearts in rage still beat for our salvation—
Oh soldiers, sewn by death, your noble lover,
in our old furrows you regenerate!

You, whose life-blood washed our soiled standards red,
the dead of Valmy, Italy, Fleurus,
thousands of Christs, red-bonnetted . . . we

have let you die with our Republic, we
who lick the boots of our bored kings like dogs—
men of the Second Empire, I mean you!

IV

ON THE ROAD

I walked on the great road, my two fists lost
in my slashed pockets, and my overcoat
the ghost of a coat. Under the sky, I walked,
I was your student, Muses. What affairs

we had together! My only pants were a big hole.
Tom Thumb, the dreamer, I was knocking off
my coupled rhymes. My inn was the Great Bear;
the stars rang like silver coins in my hand.

I heard them and I squatted on my hams,
September twilight on September twilight,
rhyming into the fairy-crowded dark.

The rain's cheap wine was splashing on my face.
I plucked at the eleastics on my clobbered
shoes—one foot pressed tight against my heart.

V

AT THE GREEN CABARET

For eight days I had been knocking my boots
on the road stones. I was entering Charleroi.
At the Green Cabaret, I called for ham,
half cold, and a large helping of tartines.

Happy, I kicked my shoes off, cooled my feet
under the table, green like the room, and laughed
at the naive Belgian pictures on the wall.
But it was terrific when the house-girl

with her earth-mother tits and come-on eyes—
no Snow Queen having cat-fits at a kiss—
brought me tarts and ham on a colored plate.

She stuck a clove of garlic in the ham,
red frothed by white, and slopped beer in my stein—
foam gilded by a ray of the late sun.

VI

A MALICIOUS GIRL

In the cigar-brown dining room, perfumed
by a smell of shellac and cabbage soup,
I held my plate and raked together some
God-awful Belgian dish. I blew my soup,

and listened to the clock tick while I ate,
and then the kitchen opened with a blast;
a housemaid entered, God knows why—her blouse
half open, yellow hair in strings. She touched

a little finger trembling to her cheek,
where the peach-velvet changed from white to red,
and made a schoolgirl grimace with her lips . . .

She swept away the plates to clear my mind,
then—just like that—quite sure of being kissed,
she whispered, "Look, my cheek has caught a cold."

VII

THE SLEEPER IN THE VALLEY

The swollen river sang through the green hole,
and madly hooked white tatters on the grass.
Light escaladed the hot hills. The whole
valley bubbled with sunbeams like a beer-glass.

The conscript was open-mouthed; his bare head
and neck swam in the bluish water cress.
He slept. The mid-day soothed his heaviness,
sunlight was raining into his green bed,

and baked the bruises from his body, rolled
as a sick child might hug itself asleep . . .
Oh Nature, rock him warmly, he is cold.

The flowers no longer make his hot eyes weep.
The river sucks his hair. His blue eye rolls.
He sleeps. In his right side are two red holes.

VIII

EVIL

All day the red spit of the chain-shot tore
whistling across the infinite blue sky,
while the great captain saw his infantry
flounder in massed battalions into fire.

The criminal injustice that deceives
and rules us, lays our corpses end on end,
then burns us like the summer grass or leaves;
La Patrie is avaricious to this end!

She is a god that laughs at Papal bulls,
the great gold chalice and the thuribles.
She dozes while our grand hosannas drown

the guns and drums, and wakes to hear the grief
of widows or a mother who lays down
her great sou knotted in a handkerchief.

Rimbaud: *L'éclatante victoire; Rages
de Césars; Morts de quatre-vingt-douze;
Ma Bohème; Au cabaret vert; La ma-
line; Le dormeur du val; Le mal.*

The Lice-Hunters

The child, feverish, frowning, only saw red
finally, and begged the fairies for his life;
the royal sisters sat beside his bed;
each long and silver finger was a knife.

They laid the child beside the window's arch,
half-open. A glass of violets drank the blue;
he felt their wicked razor fingers march
through his thick hair to comb away the dew.

He heard their singing breath, and tried to breathe
the scent of rose and almond honey, hissed
and whistled through the fissures of their teeth,
sucking saliva from the lips he kissed.

He heard their eyebrows beating in the dark
whenever an electric finger struck to crush
a bloated louse, and blood would pop and mark
the indolence of their disdainful touch.

Wine of idleness had flushed his eyes;
somewhere a child's harmonica pushed its sigh
insanely through the wearied lungs—the rise
and dying of his ceaseless wish to cry.

Rimbaud: *Les chercheuses de poux.*

At Gautier's Grave

To you, gone emblem of man's happiness,
health! Do not think I raise this empty cup
and insane toast to nothingness, because
the non-existent corridor gives hope.
A golden monster suffers on the stem;
your apparition cannot comfort me,
I myself sealed you in your porphyry,
Gautier! The rite is for my hands to dash
their torch against your vault's thick iron gate.
We, who are here simply to celebrate
the absence of the poet, must confess
his sepulcher encloses him entire,
unless the burning glory of his craft,
a window where the light is proud to flash,
answer the mortal sun's pure fire with fire—
ashes to ashes in the common draft!

Marvelous, total, and alone, your boast
was such as false pride trembles to exhale—
that crowd already changing to the pale,
opaque unbeing of its future ghost.
But when fake mourning drapes the blazoned bier,
if one of these dead poets should appear,
serene, deaf even to my sacred verse,
and pass, the guest of his vague shroud, to be
the virgin hero of posterity—
I scorn the lucid horror of a tear.

A vast hole carried by a mass of fog,
the angry wind of words he did not say,
nothingness questions the abolished man:
the dream shrieks, "Say what the earth was, you,
its shadow! Space has no answer but this toy,
this voice whose clearness falters, 'I don't know.'"

The master, just by gazing, can reclaim
the restless miracle of paradise.
Once his voice alone was the final frisson
that gave the lily and the rose their name.
Does anything remain of this great claim?
No. Men, forget your narrow faiths, no shade
darkens our métier's artificial fire.

Thinking of you, I call on you: Remain—
Oh lost now in the gardens of this Star—
honor the calm disaster of our earth:
with drunken red words from the loving cup,
a solemn agitation on the air
the crystal gaze of diamonds and rain,
that falls, unfading, on the wilted flower,
the isolation of its sunlit hour.

His tombstone ornaments the garden path—
here is the only true and lasting light,
where the poet's casual, humble gesture ends
the dream that murders his humanity;
today on the great morning of his sleep,
when ancient death is now, as with Gautier,
only the closing of his sacred eyes,
a chance for patience, we too stand and see
this solid sepulcher holds all that hurt:
miserly silence and the massive night.

Mallarmé: *Toast funèbre.*

Helen

I am the blue! I come from the lower world
to hear the serene erosion of the surf;
once more I see the galleys bleed with dawn,
and shark with muffled rowlocks into Troy.
My solitary hands recall the kings;
I used to run my fingers through their beards;
I wept. They sang about their shady wars,
the great gulfs boiling sternward from their keels.
I hear the military trumpets, all that brass,
blasting commands to the frantic oars;
the rowers' metronome enchains the sea,
and high on beaked and dragon prows, the gods—
their fixed, archaic smiles stung by the salt—
reach out their carved, indulgent arms to me!

Valéry: *Hélène.*

A Roman Sarcophagus

The terrible Etruscan mater familias
with her lethal smile
and the reddish dust of her toga
still lounges at ease
like Madame Récamier on her tomb-lid

In the beginning how familiar
the whirling water
of her pleats growing water-smooth
under the pressure of the breasts
spread like ox-horns!

What hinders our supposing
such arrest, posing and dominance
are momentary
once the corpse loses
its technicolor beauty?

Among the bangles, pious pictures, bits of glass,
this sarcophagus
once cradled something
gradually disintegrating
in a slowly dirtying slip.

Then the stone slopped it down.
Where's the intelligence
to galvanize this dead presence,
to put her to use
just once?

That would be water
glittering like geysers,
the tarpon's or marlin's mermaid flash,
water delivered
from the imperial aqueducts.

Rilke: *Römische Sarkophage.*

The Cadet Picture of My Father

(For Viola Bernard)

There's absence in the eyes. The brow's in touch
with something far. Now distant boyishness
and seduction shadow his enormous lips,
the slender aristocratic uniform
with its Franz Josef braid; both the hands bulge
like gloves upon the saber's basket hilt.
The hands are quiet, they reach out toward nothing—
I hardly see them now, as if they were
the first to grasp distance and disappear,
and all the rest lies curtained in itself,
and so withdrawn, I cannot understand
my father as he bleaches on this page—

Oh quickly disappearing photograph
in my more slowly disappearing hand!

Rilke: *Jugend-Bildnis meines Vaters.*

Self-Portrait

The bone-build of the eyebrows has a mule's
or Pole's noble and narrow steadfastness.
A scared blue child is peering through the eyes,
and there's a kind of weakness, not a fool's,
yet womanish—the gaze of one who serves.
The mouth is just a mouth . . . untidy curves,
quite unpersuasive, yet it says its *yes,*
when forced to act. The forehead cannot frown
and likes the shade of dumbly looking down.

A still life, *nature morte*—hardly a whole!
It has done nothing worked through or alive,
in spite of pain, in spite of comforting . . .
Out of this distant and disordered thing
something in earnest labors to unroll.

Rilke: *Selbstbildnis aus dem Jahre 1906.*

Orpheus, Eurydice and Hermes

(For William Meredith)

That's the strange regalia of souls.
Vibrant
as platinum filaments they went,
like arteries through their darkness. From the holes
of powder beetles, from the otter's bed,
from the oak king judging by the royal oak—
blood like our own life-blood, sprang.
Otherwise nothing was red.

The dark was heavier than Caesar's foot.

There were canyons there,
distracted forests, and bridges over air-pockets;
a great gray, blind lake
mooned over the background canals,
like a bag of winds over the Caucasus.
Through terraced highlands, stocked with cattle and patience,
streaked the single road.
It was unwinding like a bandage.

They went on this road.

First the willowy man in the blue cloak;
he didn't say a thing. He counted his toes.
His step ate up the road,
a yard at a time, without bruising a thistle. His hands fell,
clammy and clenched,
as if they feared the folds of his tunic,
as if they didn't know a thing about the frail lyre,
hooked on his left shoulder,
like roses wrestling an olive tree.

It was as though his intelligence were cut in two.
His outlook worried like a dog behind him,
now diving ahead, now romping back,
now yawning on its haunches at an elbow of the road.
What he heard breathed myrrh behind him,
and often it seemed to reach back to them,
those two others
on oath to follow behind to the finish.
Then again there was nothing behind him,
only the backring of his heel,
and the currents of air in his blue cloak.
He said to himself, "For all that, they are there."
He spoke aloud and heard his own voice die.
"They are coming, but if they are two,
how fearfully light their step is!"
Couldn't he turn round? (Yet a single back-look
would be the ruin of this work
so near perfection.) And as a matter of fact,
he knew he must now turn to them, those two light ones,
who followed and kept their counsel.

First the road-god, the messenger man . . .
His caduceus shadow-bowing behind him,
his eye arched, archaic,
his ankles feathered like arrows—
in his left hand he held *her,*
the one so loved that out of a single lyre
more sorrow came than from all women in labor,
so that out of this sorrow came
the fountain-head of the world: valleys, fields,
towns, roads . . . acropolis,
marble quarries, goats, vineyards.
And this sorrow-world circled about her,
just as the sun and stern stars
circle the earth—
a heaven of anxiety ringed by the determined stars . . .
that's how *she* was.

She leant, however, on the god's arm;
her step was delicate from her wound—
uncertain, drugged and patient.
She was drowned in herself, as in a higher hope,
and she didn't give the man in front of her a thought,
nor the road climbing to life.
She was in herself. Being dead
fulfilled her beyond fulfillment.
Like an apple full of sugar and darkness,
she was full of her decisive death,
so green she couldn't bite into it.
She was still in her marble maidenhood,
untouchable. Her sex had closed house,
like a young flower rebuking the night air.

Her hands were still ringing and tingling—
even the light touch of the god
was almost a violation.

A woman?
She was no longer that blond transcendence
so often ornamenting the singer's meters,
nor a hanging garden in his double bed.
She had wearied of being the hero's one possession.

She was as bountiful as uncoiled hair,
poured out like rain,
shared in a hundred pieces like her wedding cake.

She was a root, self-rooted.

And when the god suddenly gripped her,
and said with pain in his voice, "He is looking back at us,"
she didn't get through to the words,
and answered vaguely, "Who?"

Far there, dark against the clear entrance,
stood some one, or rather no one
you'd ever know. He stood and stared
at the one level, inevitable road,
as the reproachful god of messengers
looking round, pushed off again.
His caduceus was like a shotgun on his shoulder.

Rilke: *Orpheus, Eurydike, Hermes*

Winter Noon

At the moment when I was still happy
(God forgive me my bombast!)
who punctured my brief joy?
You'll say a Milanese blond
passing by, who laughed at me.
No, it was a balloon,
a sky-blue balloon drifting
through the blue of the winter noon.
The Italian heaven was never so blue:
there were puffy white clouds,
the sun burned the house-windows,
a string of smoke slipped
from one or two chimneys,
when the balloon took flight
over all things, all those divine things,
and escaped the inconsiderate hand
of the boy—(Surely he was weeping
in the middle of that crush
for his sorrow, his terrible sorrow)
between the Stock Exchange
and the Coffee House,
where I was killing time,
as I gaped at his balloon,
dipping and lifting . . .

Saba: *Mezzogiorno d'inverno.*

You Knocked Yourself Out

I

Those unnumbered, ruthless, random stones,
tense, vibrating still, as if slung
by the smothered abysmal fire;
the terror of those Amazon cataracts cascading
down miles to the chaos of implacable embraces;
the rock's lockjaw above the sand's
detonating dazzle—do you remember?

The sky-line, a blinding china saucer?

Do you remember the mountain, that wounded giantess?
The stranded sand-pine
with its nets of roots as mineral as the shards they finger,
as it beetled above the down-slope, only
yawning to engulf the horizon shadows?
Cool that grotto's gullet filled
with salad leaves and butterflies—
do you remember it, dumb, delirious,
there just under the summit's rotunda stone,
three men's length tall?
A king-pin of flint, teetering,
immobile?

Quick wren. Greedy eyes drunk with wonder.
You zig-zagged from fiber to fiber
to conquer the height's speckled crown,
dare-devil, musical child,
and loitered there alone to spy into the lapis lazuli bayou,
where unearthly, moss-browed turtles
were rousing from the ooze.

There the tension of nature at its lowest,
submarine sublimities,
nihilist admonitions!

II

You lifted arms like wings,
and gave the winds back their youth,
as you ran on the inertia of the stock-still air.

No one ever saw
your deft foot rest from the dance.

III

Lucky grace,
how could you help knocking your brains out
on such horny blindness—
you, simple breath, crystal bubble,

a candle, too dazzling
for the shaggy, random, vandalistic
burning of the naked sun!

Ungaretti: *Tu ti spezzasti.*

Dora Markus

It was where a plank pier
pushed from Porto Corsini into the open sea;
a handful of men, dull as blocks, drop,
draw in their nets. With a toss
of your thumb, you point out the other shore,
invisible, your true country.
Then we trailed a canal to the outlying shipyards,
silvered with sun and soot—
a patch of town-sick country, where depressed spring,
full of amnesia, was burning out.

Here where the old world's way of surviving
is subtilized by a nervous
Levantine anxiety,
your words flash a rainbow,
like the scales of a choking mullet.

Your restlessness makes me think
of migratory birds diving at a lighthouse
on an ugly night—
even your ennui is a whirlwind,
circling invisibly—
the let-ups non-existent.
I don't know how, so pressed, you've stood up
to that puddle of diffidence, your heart.

What saves you, perhaps,
is a charm, which you keep
near your lipstick, puff and nail-file—
a white mouse made of ivory . . .
Thus you exist.

[1926]

II

In your own Carinthia now
your corsage is the crescent
hedges of flowering myrtle . . .
You sashay on the curb of a stagnant pond,
and watch the timid carp swallowing, swallowing,
or saunter under the lime trees,
and follow the kindling night
along the frowzy shorefront.
The purple and orange awnings of landings
and *pensioni* throw
a bonfire on the water.

Night blanketing
the fogging lake coves
brings only the catcalls of geese,
the put-put-put of the outboards.
The snow-white majolicas of your interior
have seen you alter,
and tell your fly-blown mirror
a story of cool miscalculations,
now engraved where no sponge can expunge.

That's your legend, Dora!
But it is written already
on the moist lips of sugar daddies
with weak, masculine side-burns,
in the ten inch gold frames
of the grand hotels—
it lives in the asthma
of the sprung harmonica
at the hour when daylight muddies, each day later.

It is written there!
The evergreen laurel lives on
for the kitchen, the voice doesn't change;
Ravenna is far away. A ferocious faith
distills its venom.
What does it want from you?
Not that you surrender
voice, legend or destiny . . .

[1939]

Montale: *Dora Markus.*

Day and Night

A feather floating from a feather-duster
can sketch your figure, or a sunbeam playing
hide and seek on my typescript, or the blinding semaphore
of a child's mirror, or a skylight on a roof.
Along the brick wall, knobby as a crocodile,
scrolls of vapor
prolong the steeple-tops of the poplars;
out on the sidewalk the hurdy-gurdy man's
ruffled parrot takes umbrage.
The night is like the sultry sulphur of Montecatini
on the little squares, on the footsteps; and always
this merciless parole for taking one's measure
in order to rise to the heroism of the quotidian,
the myopia of the incubus or succubus that cannot catch
the light of your eyes in the incandescent cave;
and always the same Saturday night ulcer of the multiplying family;
and the cancerous belly-aching on the veranda,
if a shotgun go off and redden your throat
and scatter your feathers,
Oh imperiled bird of the dawn . . .
And the hospitals and cloisters wake
to the reveille of military concerts.

Montale: *Giorno e notte.*

The Magnolia's Shadow

The shadow of the dwarf magnolia
is a scarecrow now that the turkey-wattle
blossoms are blown. Like something wired,
the cicada vibrates at timed intervals.
It is no longer the Easter of voices in unison,
Clizia, the season of the infinite deity,
who devours his faithful, then revives them in blood.
It was more facile to expend one's self,
and die at the first wing-flutter, at the first
hectic rumbling from the adversary—a nursery game.
The hard way begins now; but not for you,
eaten by sunlight, rooted—yet a fragile thrush,
flying high over those frogskin mudbanks,
not for you to whom zenith, nadir, capricorn
and cancer rush together, so that the war may be
inside you, and in your adorer, who sees on you
the stigmata of the Bridegroom—the shiver
of snowfall doesn't jar you. Others
shy backwards and hold back. The artisan's
subtle file shall be silent; the hollow husk
of the singer shall be powdered glass
under your feet; the shadow is neutral.
It's autumn, it's winter, it's the other
side of the sky, that leads you—there

I break water, a fish left high and dry
under the new moon.
Goodbye.

Montale: *L'ombra della magnolia.*

Hitlerian Spring

A dense white cold of maddened moths
swaggers past parapet and lamp,
shaking a sheet upon the earth,
crackling like sugar underfoot.
Now the new season—
the nearing summer liberates
the thaw and chill
from stoneyard, lumberyard and orchard,
wood tossed by the river to its banks.

(An infernal possessor
motorcycles down the Corso;
hurrahing stooges and a jangle
of hooked crosses absorb and swallow
him—a thunderhead of light!)

                        The old shop
windows are shuttered, poor and harmless,
though even these are armed with cannon
and toys of war. This spring, the butcher
locks his creaking iron curtain—
once he would hook two goat's-heads crowned
with holly berries on his door . . .
they were a kind of ritual for
those mild young killers, unaware
the blood they spilled had been transformed

to a sick mangle of crushed wings.
Here barnacles and old mortgages
keep chiselling at the river-piles—
and no one, ahi, now is blameless!

The sirens and the tolling bells . . .
For nothing, then? On Saint John's Day,
the stinking roman candles scour
the air. Once more, spring! Now the slow
farewell, as sad as Baptism,
the mournful vigil of the horde,
the head brought in upon a board,
now diamond powder blurs the air,
and shakes down ice—the sky is like
Tobias looking at the sky,
seeing the seven seraphs flame.
Light rays and seeds are drifting down
through pollen hissing into fire,
through crushed and crooked fingers,
through the sharpness of driving snow,
the sirens and the tolling bells . . .

Clizia,
April's reopened wound is raw! . . .

Montale: *La primavera hitleriana.*

The Coastguard House

A death-cell? The shack of the coastguards
is a box over the drop to the breakers;
it waits for you without an owner,
ever since the mob of your thoughts
bullied a welcome,
and stayed on there, unrequited.
You didn't take it to heart.

For years the sirocco gunned the dead stucco with sand;
the sound of your laugh is a jagged coughing;
the compass, a pin-head, spins at random;
the dizzy dice screw up the odds.
You haven't taken my possession to heart;
another time has thinned your nostalgia;
a thread peels from the spool.

I hold an end of it,
but the house balks backward;
its sea-green weathercock
creaks and caws without pity.
I keep one end of the thread,
but you house alone
and hold your hollow breath there in the dark.

Oh the derelict horizon,
sunless except for the
orange hull of a lonely, drudging tanker!
The breakers bubble on the dead-drop.
You haven't taken my one night's possession to heart;
I have no way of knowing
who forces an entrance.

Montale: *La Casa dei doganieri.*

Arsenio

Roof-high, winds worrying winds
rake up the dust, clog the chimney ventilators,
drum through the bald, distracted little squares,
where a few senile, straw-hatted horses wheeze
by the El Dorado of the rooming houses' windows in the sun.
You are like an acid clash of castanets
disturbing by fits and starts our workaday hours,
today, as you go down
our main street, fronting the bay—
now you are sloshed with the dreary drizzle, now you dazzle us.

It's a sign of quite another orbit: you follow it.
A gusher of lead hangs over
the ungraspable gorges, and you go down,
more rootless than the winds.
A shower of salt spray, a whirlpool,
lifts, heavy with its element rebellious to the ether.
Your step through the pebbles is a creaking,
the mop-headed, beach-tossed seaweed snags you.
Iron link in a chain! Perhaps, powerless to walk,
this moment,
you finally evade finishing your journey's
all too well publicized delirium of inaction.

Here and there among the papery palm trees
you hear the wavering outcry
of the violins, dying as the thunder slams in
with the shudder of the shops closing metal shutters.
How imposing the storm now, when Sirius sparkles
garishly against the indigo heavens, far out
where the evening is already importunate.
Like some delicate tree entering the reddening light,
lightning etches a crash of pruned branches.
The strings of the two-bit orchestra grumble for silence.

You go down to a gloom that precipitates
and changes the siesta hour into night;
globelike lanterns rock on the gunnels of fishboats
in the offing, where a single darkening presence
clasps sea and heaven. Acetylene pulses
from a few perforated, rusty funnels.

                    The sky trembles with raindrops.
The dry soil, turning to water, steams.
Everything near you is smoke,
a rustling hoes the earth,
capsizes the sopping pavilions,
douses the Chinese lanterns hissing on the esplanade.

You are flung aside
among wicker porch furniture and dank mats—
like a water-lily dragging its roots,
sticky, never sure-footed.
Hysterical with life, you stretch
towards an emptiness of suffocated sobbing.
You are knotted in the rings of the fish-net,
gulped by the gasping spent water . . .
Everything you grab hold of—
street, portico, walls and mirrors—
glues you to a paralysed crowd of dead things.

If a word fells you,
if a gesture ruins you now, Arsenio,
it's a sign that this is the hour for letting go
of the life you were always disposed to throttle.
A wind carries its ashes to the stars.

Montale: *Arsenio.*

The Chess Player

At last with stubborn jabs of your fingers
you kill the red cigarette bulb in the china dish;
expiring spirals of smoke
crinkle like lamb's fleece toward the ceiling,
and encumber the knights and bishops
on the chessboard, who hold their positions—
stupefied. Smoke-ring after smoke-ring snakes upward,
more agile than the gold mines on your fingers.

A window opens. One puff is enough
to panic the smoke's heaven-flung mirage
of imperial arches and battlements;—
down below another world moves:
a man, bruised by the sores of the wolf,
ignores your incense:
all the torture and formulae
of your small, heraldic, chessboard world.

For a time, I doubted if you yourself even
made any sense of the game, its square,
hobbled moves through gunpowder
clouds of tobacco . . . Poise cannot
pay off the folly of death; the flash
of your eyes asks that an answering crash
pierce the smoke-screen
thrown up by the god of chance to befriend you.

Today, I know what you want. I hear
the hoarse bell of the feudal campanile.
The archaic ivory chessmen are terrified.
Like snowmen, they melt in your mind's white glare.

Montale: *Nuove stanze.*

News from Mount Amiata

I

Come night,
the ugly weather's fire-cracker simmer
will deepen to the gruff buzz of beehives.
Termites tunnel the public room's rafters to sawdust,
an odor of bruised melons oozes from the floor.
A sick smoke lifts from the elf-huts and funghi of the valley—
like an eagle it climbs our mountain's bald cone,
and soils the windows.
I drag my table to the window,
and write to you—
here on this mountain, in this beehive cell
on the globe rocketed through space.
My letter is a paper hoop.
When I break through it, you will be imprisoned.

Here mildew sprouts like grass from the floor,
the canary cage is hooded with dirty green serge,
chestnuts explode on the grate.
Outside, it's raining.
There you are legendary.
Any legend falls short, if it confine you,
your gold-gated icon unfolding on gold.

II

Magnesium flares light up the hidden summits;
but the narrow feudal streets below are too dark
for the caravan of black donkeys kicking up sparks.

You are devoted to precarious
sentiments and sediment—blackened architecture;
rectangular courtyards centered
on bottomless wells. You are led
by the sinister wings of nightbirds,
the infinite pit, the luminous gape of the galaxies—
all their sleight of hand and torture.
But the step that carries out into darkness
comes from a man going alone,
who sees nothing but the nearest light-chinked shutter.
The stars' pattern is too deep for him,
atmospheric ivy only chokes his darkness,
his campanile shuts its eye at two o'clock.

III

Here on this mountain,
the world has no custom-barriers.
Let tomorrow be colder, let the north wind
shatter the stringy ribbons of old Missals,
the sandstone bastion of the barbarians.
When our sensations have no self-assurance,
everything must be a lens.
Then the polar winds will return clearer,
and convert us to our chains, the chains of the possible.

IV

Today, the monotonous oratory of the dead,
ashes, lethargic winds—
a reluctant trickle drips
from the thatched huts.
Time is water.
The rain rains down black letters—
a *contemptu mundi!* What part of me does it bring you?

Now at this late hour
of my watch and your endless, prodigal sleep,
my tiny straw city is breaking up.
The porcupine sips a quill of mercy.

                              Montale: *Notizie dall' Amiata.*

The Eel

The eel, the North Sea siren,
who leaves dead-pan Icelandic gods
and the Baltic for our Mediterranean,
our estuaries, our rivers—
who lances through their profound places,
and flinty portages, from branch to branch,
twig to twig, thinning down now,
ever snaking inward, worming
for the granite's heartland, threading
delicate capillaries of slime—
and in the Romagna one morning
the blaze of the chestnut blossoms
ignites its smudge in the dead water
pooled from chiselings
of the Apennines . . .
the eel, a whipstock, a Roman candle,
love's arrow on earth, which only
reaches the paradise of fecundity
through our gullies and fiery, charred streams;
a green spirit, potent only
where desolation and arson burn;
a spark that says everything
begins where everything is clinker;
this buried rainbow, this iris, twin sister

of the one you set in your eye's target center
to shine on the sons of men,
on us, up to our gills in your life-giving mud—
can you call her *Sister?*

II

If they called you a fox,
it will be for your monstrous hurtle,
your sprint that parts and unites,
that kicks up and freshens the gravel,
(your black lace balcony, overlooking
the home for deformed children, a meadow,
and a tree, where my carved name quivers,
happy, humble, defeated)—
or perhaps only for the phosphorescent wake
of your almond eyes,
for the craft of your alert panic,
for the annihilation of dishevelled feathers
in your child's hand's python hug;
if they have likened you to the blond lioness,
to the avaricious demon of the undergrowth
(and why not to the filthy fish
that electrocutes, the torpedo fish?)
it is perhaps because the blind
have not seen the wings
on your delectable shoulder-blades,
because the blind haven't shot for
your forehead's luminous target,
the furrow I pricked there in blood,
cross, chrism, incantation,—and
prayer—damnation, salvation;

if they can only think of you
as a weasel or a woman,
with whom can I share my discovery,
where bury the gold I carry,
the red-hot, pot-bellied furnace raging
inside me, when, leaving me,
you turn up stairs?

Montale: *L'anguilla; Se t'hanno assomigliato.*

Little Testament

This thing the night flashes
like marshlight through the skull of my mind,
this pearl necklace snail's trail,
this ground glass, diamond-dust sparkle—
it is not the lamp in any church or office,
tended by some adolescent altar boy,
Communist or papist,
in black or red.
I have only this rainbow
to leave you, this testimonial
of a faith, often invaded,
of a hope that burned more slowly
than a green log on the fire.
Keep its spectrum in your pocket-mirror,
when every lamp goes out,
when hell's orchestra trembles,
and the torch-bearing Lucifer
lands on some bowsprit
in the Thames, Hudson or Seine—
rotating his hard coal wings,
half lopped by fatigue, to tell you, "Now."
It's hardly an heirloom or charm
that can tranquillize monsoons
with the transparent spider web of contemplation—
but an autobiography can only survive in ashes,
persistence is extinction.

It is certainly a sign: whoever has seen it,
will always return to you.
Each knows his own: his pride
was not an escape, his humility
was not a meanness, his obscure
earth-bound flash
was not the fizzle of a wet match.

Montale: *Piccolo testamento*.

Black Spring

A half-holiday for the burial. Of course, they punish
the provincial copper bells for hours;
terribly the nose tilts up like a tallow candle
from the coffin. Does it wish to draw breath
from its torso in a mourning suit? The last snow
fell somberly—white, then the roads were bread-crumbed with pebbles.
Poor winter, honeycombed with debts,
poured to corruption. Now the dumb, black springtime
must look into the chilly eye . . . from under the mould
on the roof-shingles, the liquid oatmeal
of the roads, the green stubble of life
on our faces! High in the splinter elm,
shrill the annual fledglings with their spikey necks.
They say to man that his road is mud,
his luck is rutted—there is nothing
sorrier than the marriage of two deaths.

Annensky.

September

The much-hugged rag-doll is oozing cotton from her ruined figure.
Unforgetting September cannot hide its peroxide curls of leaf.
Isn't it time to board up the summer house?
The carpenter's gavel pounds for new and naked roof-ribs.

The moment the sun rises, it disappears.
Last night the marsh by the swimming pool shivered with fever;
the last bell-flowers waste under the rheumatic dewdrop,
a dirty lilac stain souses the birches.

The woods are discomforted. The animals
head for the snow-stopped bear holes in the fairy tales;
behind the black park fences, tree trunks and pillars
form columns like a newspaper's death column.

The thinning birchwood has not ceased to water its color—
more and more watery, its once regal shade.
Summer keeps mumbling, "I am only a few months old.
A lifetime of looking back, what shall I do with it?

"I've so many mind-bruises, I should give up playing.
They are like birds in the bushes, mushrooms on the lawn.
Now we have begun to paper our horizon with them
to fog out each other's distance."

Stricken with polio, Summer, *le roi soleil,*
hears the gods' Homeric laughter from the dignitaries' box—
with the same agony, the country house
stares forward, hallucinated, at the road to the metropolis.

Pasternak.

For Anna Akmatova

It seems I am choosing words that will stand,
and you are in them,
but if I blunder, it doesn't matter—
I must persist in my errors.

I hear the soiled, dripping small talk of the roofs;
the students' black boots drum eclogues on the boardwalks,
the undefined city takes on personality,
is alive in each sound.

Although it's spring, there's no leaving the city.
The sharp customers overlook nothing.
You bend to your sewing until you weep;
sunrise and sunset redden your swollen eyes.

You ache for the calm reaches of Ladoga,
then hurry off to the lake for a change
of fatigue. You gain nothing,
the shallows smell like closets full of last summer's clothes.

The dry wind dances like a dried-out walnut
across the waves, across your stung eyelids—
stars, branches, milestones, lamps. A white
seamstress on the bridge is always washing clothes.

I know that objects and eyesight vary greatly
in singleness and sharpness, but the iron
heart's vodka is the sky
under the northern lights.

That's how I see your face and expression.
This, not the pillar of salt, the *Lot's Wife* you pinned down
in rhyme five years ago to show up our fear,
limping forward in blinders, afraid of looking back.

How early your first dogged, unremitting idiom
hardened—no unassembled crumbs!
In all our affairs, your lines throb
with the high charge of the world. Each wire is a conductor.

Pasternak.

Mephistopheles

Every Sunday they left a circus of dust behind them,
as they poured out on the turnpike in stately, overcrowded carriages,
and the showers found nobody at home,
and trampled through the bedroom windows.

It was a custom at these staid Sunday dinners
to serve courses of rain instead of roast-beef;
on the baroque sideboard, by the Sunday silver,
the wind cut corners like a boy on a new bicycle.

Upstairs, the curtain rods whirled, untouched;
the curtains rose like a salvo to the ceiling.
Outside the burghers kept losing themselves,
they showed up chewing straws by cow-ponds.

Later, when the long cortege of carriages
approached the city wall,
the horses shied
from the shadow of the Gothic gallows.

The devil in blood-red stockings with rose rosettes
danced along the sunset-watered road—
he was as red,
as a boiling lobster.

One thought a snort of indignation
had ripped the lid of heaven
from the skyline's low vegetation;
the devil's ribbons fluttered and danced.

The carriages swam through his eyes like road-signs;
he scarcely lifted a finger in greeting.
He rolled on his heels, he rumbled with laughter,
he sidled off hugging Faust, his pupil.

Pasternak.

The Seasons

I

Now the small buds are pronged
to the boughs like candle-butts.
Steaming April! The adolescent park
simmers.

Like a lassoed buffalo, the forest
is noosed in the ropes of shrill feathered throats—
a wrestler, all gratuitous muscle,
caught in the pipes of the grand organ.

The shadows of the young leaves are gummy.
A wet bench streams in the garden.
Poetry is like a pump
with a suction-pad that drinks and drains up

the clouds. They ruffle in hoop-skirts,
talk to the valleys—
all night I squeeze out verses,
my page is hollow and white with thirst.

The garden's frightful—all drip and listening.
The rain is loneliness.
A branch splashes white lace on the window.
Is there a witness?

The earth is swollen and smelly,
the pasture is a sponge;
as if it were August, the far off night ripens
and rots in the elm-dissected field.

No sound. No trespasser watches the night.
The rain is alone in the garden—
it starts up again, it drips
off roof and gutter.

I will drink the rain,
I, loneliness . . .
the rain weeps in the darkness.
Is there a witness?

But silence! Not even a wrinkling leaf.
No sign in the darkness,
only a swallowing of sobs and the swish of slippers . . .
in the interval, earth choking its tears . . .

III

Summer says goodbye to the station.
Running in its photographer's black hood,
and blinding us with flash-bulbs, the thunder
takes a hundred souvenir snap-shots.

The lilac bush is a black scarecrow.
From hill and sky armfuls of lightning
crash on the station-agent's cottage
to smash it with light.

Waves of malevolence
lift the coal-dust from the roof;
the rain, coming down in buckets,
is like charcoal that smudges a drawing.

Something in my mind's
most inaccessible corners
registers the thunder's illumination,
stands up, and steadily blinks.

IV

A driving rain whips the air.
The ice is scabby gray. You wait
for the sky to wake up.
Snow drones on the wind.

With unbuckled galoshes, with a muffler
flapping from his unbuttoned coat,
March bulls ahead, and makes rushes
at the frivolous, frenzied birds.

The season cannot miss you. It tries
to scrape up the candle-drippings in a snotty handkerchief—
it is safe now
to snatch off the night-caps of the tulips . . .

He is out of his senses, he musses his mop of hair.
He is buried in his mind's mush,
and stammers scurrilities
against me—my resurrection in the spring.

V

Pinecones pop in the military gloom of our bedroom.
A gray smog boils in the overtime lightbulb.
The blue window simmers
over the snow-desert.
Our lips puff and stick.

Spring! I leave the street of astonished pines,
alarmed distances,
the awkward classical wooden house, apprehending its downfall—
the air blue as piles of faded sky-blue denim
lugged by the prisoners from their wards!

The age is breaking—pagan Rome,
thumbs down on clowns,
the wrestler's vain swansong to the grandstand—
on the true!
The overpaid gladiator must die in earnest.

Pasternak.

Sparrow Hills

Like water pouring from a pitcher, my mouth on your nipples!
Not always. The summer well runs dry.
Not for long the dust of our stamping feet, encore on encore
from the saxes in the casino's midnight gazebo.

I've heard of age—its obese warbling!
When no wave will clap hands to the stars.
If they speak, you doubt it. No face in the meadows,
no heart in the pools, no god among the pines.

Split your soul like wood. Let today froth from your mouth
It's the world's noontide. Have you no eyes for it?
Look, conception bubbles from the bleached fallows;
fir-cones, woodpeckers, clouds, pine-needles, heat

Here the city's trolley tracks give out.
Further, you must put up with peeled pine. The trolley poles are
        detached.
Further, it's Sunday. Boughs screwed loose for the picnic bonfire,
playing tag in your bra.

"The world is always like this," say the woods,
as they mix the midday glare, Whitsunday and walking.
All's planned with checkerberry couches, inspired with clearings—
the piebald clouds spill down on us like a country woman's house-dress.

Pasternak.

Wild Vines

Beneath a willow entwined with ivy,
we look for shelter from the bad weather;
one raincoat covers both our shoulders—
my fingers rustle like the wild vine around your breasts.

I am wrong. The rain's stopped.
Not ivy, but the hair of Dionysus
hangs from these willows. What am I to do?
Throw the raincoat under us!

Pasternak.

In the Woods

A lilac heat sickened the meadow;
high in the wood, a cathedral's sharp, nicked groins.
No skeleton obstructed the bodies—
all was ours, obsequious wax in our fingers . . .

Such, the dream: you do not sleep,
you only dream you thirst for sleep,
that some one elsewhere thirsts for sleep—
two black suns singe his eyelashes.

Sunbeams shower and ebb to the flow of iridescent beetles.
The dragonfly's mica whirs on your cheek.
The wood fills with meticulous scintillations—
a dial under the clockmaker's tweezers.

It seemed we slept to the tick of figures;
in the acid, amber ether,
they set up nicely tested clocks,
shifted, regulated them to a soprano hair for the heat.

They shifted them here and there, and snipped at the wheels.
Day declined on the blue clock-face;
they scattered shadows, drilled a void—
the darkness was a mast derricked upright.

It seems a green and brown happiness flits beyond us;
sleep smothers the woods;
no elegiacs on the clock's ticking—
sleep, it seems, is all this couple is up to.

Pasternak.

The Landlord

Having crossed the curb in the courtyard,
the Landlord journeyed to the feast,
into the Bride's house—

with him departed the Italian singer,
behind the Bride's weatherstripped doors,
between one and seven,

the snatches of talk had quieted down,
but the sun rose blood red in the middle of the bed—
he wanted to sleep and sleep and sleep.

The accordion began to weep,
the accordion-player lay spread out on his instrument—
hearing the palms clapping, the shuffle of the shining serfs.

The feast's whole flourish jingled like silver in his hand,
again again again again,
the song of the broken accordion.

Rustling through the bed and the sleeper,
the noise, whistling and the cheering,
swam a white peacock.

He moved his hips,
and strutted out in the street,
this beautiful bird . . .

He shook his head, he ruffled his breast-feathers;
suddenly the noise of the game
is the stamping of a whole procession.

He drops into the hole of the sun.

The sleepy courtyard grows businesslike,
mules stand up by the stone well,
teamsters shout down the laughter of the feast.

A band of pigeons
blasts from the sky's blue bowl,
as if it were following the wedding party,

as if life were only an instant, of course,
the dissolution of ourselves into others,
like a wedding party approaching the window.

                                                    Pasternak.

Hamlet in Russia, A Soliloquy

"My heart throbbed like a boat on the water.
My oars rested. The willows swayed through the summer,
licking my shoulders, elbows and rowlocks—
wait! this might happen,

when the music brought me the beat,
and the ash-gray water-lilies dragged, and a couple of daisies blew,
and a hint of blue dotted a point off-shore—
lips to lips, stars to stars!

My sister, life!
the world has too many people for us,
the sycophant, the spineless—
politely, like snakes in the grass, they sting.

My sister!
embrace the sky and Hercules
who holds the world up forever
at ease, perhaps, and sleeps at night

thrilled by the nightingales crying . . .

The boat stops throbbing on the water . . .

The clapping stops. I walk into the lights
as Hamlet, lounge like a student against the door-frame,
and try to catch the far-off dissonance of life—
all that has happened, and must!

From the dark the audience leans its one hammering brow against me—
ten thousand opera glasses, each set on the tripod!
Abba, Father, all things are possible with thee—
take away this cup!

I love the mulishness of Providence,
I am content to play the one part I was born for . . .
quite another play is running now . . .
take me off the hooks tonight!

The sequence of scenes was well thought out;
the last bow is in the cards, or the stars—
but I am alone, and there is none . . .
All's drowned in the sperm and spittle of the Pharisee—

To live a life is not to cross a field."

Pasternak.

Pigeons

(For Hannah Arendt)

The same old flights, the same old homecomings,
dozens of each per day,
but at last the pigeon gets clear of the pigeon-house . . .
What is home, but a feeling of homesickness
for the flight's lost moment of fluttering terror?

Back in the dovecote, there's another bird,
by all odds the most beautiful,
one that never flew out, and can know nothing of gentleness . . .
Still, only by suffering the rat-race in the arena
can the heart learn to beat.

Think of Leonidas perhaps and the hoplites,
glittering with liberation,
as they combed one another's golden Botticellian hair
at Thermopylae, friends and lovers, the bride and the bridegroom—
and moved into position to die.

Over non-existence arches the all-being—
thence the ball thrown almost out of bounds
stings the hand with the momentum of its drop—
body and gravity,
miraculously multiplied by its mania to return.

Rilke: *Die Tauben.*